International Studies in the Next Millennium

International Studies in the Next Millennium

Meeting the Challenge of Globalization

Julia A. Kushigian, Editor
Penny Parsekian, Assistant Editor

Under the auspices of
The Toor Cummings Center,
Connecticut College

Westport, Connecticut
London

Library of Congress Cataloging-in-Publication Data

International studies in the next millennium : meeting the challenge
of globalization / Julia A. Kushigian, editor ; Penny Parsekian,
assistant editor ; under the auspices of The Toor Cummings Center,
Connecticut College.
     p.   cm.
   Selected papers from a conference on "The future of international
studies in the liberal arts context" led by The Toor Cummings Center
for International Studies and the Liberal Arts at Connecticut
College in June 1996.
   Includes bibliographical references and index.
   ISBN 0–275–96045–5 (alk. paper)
    1. International education—Congresses. 2. Education, Humanistic—
Congresses. 3. Education, Higher—Curricula—Congresses.
4. Education, Higher—Aims and objectives—Congresses.
I. Kushigian, Julia Alexis. II. Parsekian, Penny. III. Toor
Cummings Center for International Studies and the Liberal Arts
(Connecticut College)
LC1090.I579   1998
378'.01—DC21   97–22807

British Library Cataloguing in Publication Data is available.

Library of Congress Catalog Card Number: 97–22807
ISBN: 0–275–96045–5

First published in 1998

Praeger Publishers, 88 Post Road West, Westport, CT 06881
An imprint of Greenwood Publishing Group, Inc.

Printed in the United States of America

The paper used in this book complies with the
Permanent Paper Standard issued by the National
Information Standards Organization (Z39.48–1984).

10 9 8 7 6 5 4 3 2 1

Copyright Acknowledgments

The editors and the publisher gratefully acknowledge permission for use of
the following material:

From the book *Kokoro* by Natsume Soseki. Edwin McClellan translation Copyright © 1957; reprinted © 1996. All rights reserved. Reprinted by special permission of Regnery Publishing, Inc., Washington, D.C.

Excerpts from "The Waste Land" by T. S. Eliot. *Collected Poems, 1909–1962*.
London: Faber and Faber Ltd.

Contents

Acknowledgments

I wish to express my gratitude to the Henry B. Luce Foundation and the William and Flora Hewlett Foundation for their support of the conference, "The Future of International Studies in the Liberal Arts Context," held at Connecticut College in June 1996. The conference was the source of the essays in this volume.

I also wish to express my appreciation to Suzanne Cleworth-Jones for her persistence and creativity in organizing the conference and to Sarabeth Fields for her dedication and fine work in the preparation of the manuscript for publication.

Introduction

Julia A. Kushigian

In June 1996, the Toor Cummings Center for International Studies and the Liberal Arts at Connecticut College lead a conference on "The Future of International Studies in the Liberal Arts Context," the goal of which was to explore international studies on both a theoretical and practical level. Fifty-seven colleges and universities from the United States, France, and Japan sent teams that included faculty and administrators. Participants sought to understand the external forces that compel us to think internationally, instead of locally or nationally, and to discover why the best thinking of this nature can be reached within the liberal arts tradition. It was our goal to recognize the conceptual forces that make inevitable the push of modernity toward internationalization and the pull of tradition toward culture and ethnicity. We also examined common challenges and unique responses based on budgetary, curricular, and ideological differences.

As healthy, dynamic institutions, we all approached the topic from different perspectives. Some were just beginning to lay the groundwork for pursuing international studies, while others had established programs/majors and had received significant financial support for their efforts. Whatever the status of the international studies debate on the individual campus, each team was willing to test its theoretical approach and consider the practical suggestions of others. The present volume is a compilation of chapters selected from the papers and workshops given at the conference. The selection represents the intellectual debate, from a variety of complementary perspectives, on international studies as conceived and taught in liberal arts institutions today.

The effort to center the debate of international studies in the liberal arts tradition stems from three related conditions: first, the struggle of liberal arts institutions against the forces that would marginalize the humanities as being too impractical; second, the joy of lifelong learning grounded in the marriage of critical skills and moral judgment as found in the liberal arts tradition, which calls upon us to use our learning for the common good; and third, the possibility to create "public intellectuals" from all walks of life who will strive for the common good.

Historically, the greatest challenge for all institutions is to address phenomena on a local, campus level, while viewing this as a microcosm of what occurs internationally. The challenge for us is to resolve the tension between internationalization/globalization on the one hand and localization/traditionalization on the other. The debate is between homogenization and diversity. The dichotomy between transcending national boundaries (seen in shrinking markets, international banking systems, and regional trade agreements) and upholding national boundaries (seen in ethnic, cultural, religious, gender, language, and land-related ties that bind) fuels this debate. In the national debate, it has been reconfigured as a question of the West against the rest—whether globalization equals the shrinking of opposites through similar markets and macro trends as posited by Benjamin Barber, or whether globalization is capable or incapable of promoting a universal culture as pondered by Samuel P. Huntington. At institutes of higher learning, this dichotomy translates into the tension or disjuncture between internationalization and area studies.

The present volume begins with a part on "The Academy and International Studies" that provides an extraordinary composition by Tu Wei-ming, "Mustering the Conceptual Resources to Grasp a World in Flux." This chapter concludes that we are in need of a new way of perceiving predicated on a radically transformed world view. In essence, according to Tu Wei-ming, globalization does not mean homogenization. It should not be considered an either/or proposition, but a both/and opportunity. That is, the problems of ethnicity, language, gender, land, class, and faith should be used to challenge the interdependence of the global community. Furthermore, this fruitful debate can and should be conducted by public intellectuals who are "politically concerned, socially engaged, and culturally sensitive and informed." Tu Wei-ming concludes that the public intellectual trained at the liberal arts institution must play an important role in academics, government, business, and civic and religious organizations, as well as in significant movements such as social, environmental, human rights, feminist, and philanthropic.

In "The Liberal Arts Role: Cultivating a Common Ethic of Care," Peter S. Thacher speaks to the importance of mobilizing international leadership and funds to assist all, including developing countries, to serve the common good ecologically. He explains that agreements, protocols, and treaties to curb human actions that would otherwise have life-threatening consequences for the entire planet are predicated on common values. Thacher credits a multidisciplinary approach to problem solving—which is the heart of the liberal arts tradition—operating at the international level, while coming to grips with these threats to life on Earth. He emphasizes the need for generalists with a wide range of socioeconomic skills to help reduce poverty and other inequities in the world, holding that the major actors in this struggle are no longer limited to government agencies. They include broader representation (echoing the public intellectual of Tu Wei-ming), such as organizations of scientists, engineers, mayors, governors, women, youth, farmers, business people, parliamentarians, indigenous people, and environmentalists.

Claire L. Gaudiani, in her chapter, "Tossed into a New Frame: Learning before Teaching," focuses on the problem of how to teach students not to simply be followers of systems, but transformers and creators of more just democracies, economies, and prosperous societies for all citizens. She recognizes the power of the liberal arts tradition to teach us across cultures and time about who we are as human beings. Furthermore, she underscores its ethical framework as the broad structure within which we examine political, economic, and social systems. Employing the example of the Mexican government's protracted conflict in 1994-95 with the indigenous Zapatistas as a striking case of global interdependence, Gaudiani drives home the importance of educators retraining themselves before making changes on their campuses. True to the liberal arts paradigm, she makes the point that we are all connected, not only by the global market, but to each other's well-being.

In "Synthesis and Tension: Creating an International Studies Program," Robert E. Proctor sets forth the task of how to put the liberal arts vision within a modern international context. He explores the three educational traditions—liberal arts, utilitarian, and research—and addresses the challenges of how to apply international studies to a liberal arts context, as well as how to put the major into an international, broader interdisciplinary context (a challenge for faculty and students alike). Proctor delineates the idea of self-transcendence, of rising above self-interest and working for the common good, which emanates from the liberal arts tradition and views each discipline as a complementary way of understanding the whole.

In Part Two, entitled "Dynamic Models: Pedagogy and Programs," Neil Waters and David Macey introduce a chapter, "Beyond the Area Studies Wars," that takes an innovative look at a complex problem. It explores the tension between international and area studies as fundamental in the movement to internationalize our campuses. The compromise they developed to satisfy both globally-oriented theorists and area studies specialists entails a new major in international studies that combines the narrowly-focused strengths of an area studies major (cultural specificity, foreign language, regional study) with the broader, comparative, thematic, and cross-regional perspectives of international studies programs. Ultimately, they seek to impart to students a deep understanding of a specific geographical region and language, as well as its place within an interdisciplinary and transnational context.

Julia A. Kushigian's chapter, "Reaching Moral and Cultural Maturity through International Studies," focuses on the need to incorporate ethical concerns in a foundation of critical skills and international studies. In seeking a common set of values, the Connecticut College Program embodies a liberal arts education for the twenty-first century, permitting all majors to be internationalized with a base in the liberal arts. It encourages students to unite critical skills with moral concerns to help them translate complex ideas from their fields into everyday metaphors in English as well as a foreign language. By asking area studies to support internationalization, we encourage a healthy tension that promotes cross-cultural communications, cross-regional debate, foreign language, and cultural maturity. The result is that students design their area studies; take globally oriented seminars that ask them to debate material, spiritual, and ethical challenges to internationalization; complete overseas internships in the foreign language and culture; and complete projects that integrate international studies and the major to become globally responsible citizen leaders.

The chapter contributed by Joan O'Mara, Jane Horvath, Marcia Seabury, Harald Sandstrom, and Susan Coleman, "The All-University Curriculum: A Team-Teaching, Interdisciplinary, and Inter-College Approach," describes a tactical approach to the internationalization of the curriculum at the University of Hartford. Their all-university curriculum includes interdisciplinary and team-taught courses from five different categories and explores living in cultural and social contexts, as well as in a scientific and technological world. Their formula for internationalization, which is a strategic goal of the university, addresses international and global issues within a competitive framework. Their ability to have the curriculum accepted by the faculty and the administration rested on the internationalization of those existing courses that lent themselves to international perspectives, rather than creating new courses. They conclude that the most rewarding aspects of their courses is that students gain an understanding of what it means to be citizens of the world and how much their actions affect others.

M. Kathleen Mahnke, Kathleen Rupright, and Bonnie Tangalos contributed a chapter entitled "Weaving International Perspectives into the Fabric of a College Community," which explores the redesigning of the academic structure of St. Michael's College to meet the changing needs of the college and its student body. In 1987 they integrated the School of International Studies (SIS) into the academic structure and community of the college. New course models were developed by the faculty in the SIS and the Department of Modern Languages for both domestic and international students. The courses build on language skills and increased awareness of other cultures and disciplines. In addition, St. Michael's strength lies in a dynamic model of long-term planning that will establish links with educational institutions worldwide to facilitate faculty and student exchanges, as well as cooperative programming.

In Part Three, "Language Proficiency Revisited," Denise Rochat and Margaret Skiles Zelljadt address a recurring concern about study-away programs with a resourceful solution. Their chapter, "Beyond Accidental Tourism: The Case for a Junior Year Abroad," makes a strong argument for a year-long study abroad program. Smith College offers such programs in France, Germany, Italy, and Switzerland, and 30 percent of Smith students study abroad. Rochat and Zelljadt contend that students benefit from a longer experience abroad in part because they are able to unpack psychological baggage, overcome their initial discomfort, and appreciate the experience as a formative one. Smith's specially designed orientation sessions prepare students to enroll directly in courses at the host university alongside their foreign counterparts. An essential component of the overseas experience is an internship offered in the Geneva and Hamburg programs, helping the students gain confidence in their ability to perform well in the field.

Merle Krueger's chapter, "Foreign Languages Across the Curriculum at Home and Abroad," addresses the need to boost America's competitiveness in the global marketplace, security, and quality of life by responding to developments worldwide. The focus of a successful approach at Brown is on foreign language courses extended to improve proficiency. For example, the Foreign Languages Across the Curriculum (FLAC) courses allow students to use their second languages in areas that interest them most, thereby establishing the relevance of the second language in their field. Students develop the habit of using language skills regularly as a key to learning. Apart from the successful "content" or "discipline-based" approach to language study are courses such as "French for International Relations" and intensive Italian language training that Brown offers to enhance outcomes for specialized fields.

The chapter contributed by Michael Kline and Neil Weissman, "From Serendipity to Strategy: International Education Across the Curriculum," leads a fourth and final section entitled "Breaking with Tradition: New Contexts, New Approaches." The vitality of foreign language study at Dickinson College has been reinforced by a drive toward internationalization at the college and the development of study centers abroad. Heralded for contributing to an ethos of global awareness on campus, raising academic expectations, and promoting recruiting, the nine overseas study centers act as the motor for internationalization. The centers allow the college to be wholly responsible for predeparture preparation, the abroad experience itself, and students' reintegration upon return. Making financial aid portable and overseas programs fiscally accountable allows 48 percent of the student body to study abroad without putting a burden on the general funds of the institution. The centers also encourage students to participate in internships in private industry, business, government agencies, and educational establishments. Both authors underscore the need for collegial cooperation on a small campus to accomplish a global extension of this nature. It has aided the college to secure valuable grants, initiate a new International Business and Management Program, and move beyond minimum foreign language and civilization requirements.

Nanette S. Levinson's chapter, "A 'Globaliberal' Arts Approach: The International Studies Major and the Next Millennium," explores the challenges and solutions for international studies at a major university in an international city. American University breaks new ground with a program that supports an in-depth immersion into a region's culture, the student's functional specialization, and a broad liberal arts foundation. The university's solution involves a "globaliberal" approach, which achieves the ability to see, understand, and deal with interconnections, as well as with complexity. This entails using a cross-disciplinary stance to be able to manage the multidimensional, including cultures, complexities, connections, and change.

James J. Ward and Jane Tyler Ward collaborated on the chapter, "International Studies as a Growth Strategy for a Small Liberal Arts College," which presents a creative scheme to combat the all too familiar threat of downward-spiraling enrollments and financial difficulties. Among other successful campaigns, Cedar Crest College committed itself to internationalizing the curriculum and campus life, employing materials at hand to build a program from within. Cedar Crest initiated an International Studies Co-Major Program, articulated with majors in fields such as history, politics, economics, sociology, and communications. The college also recruited students from 18 different countries, which led to the development of support systems, including English as a Second Language (ESL) programs, international buddies, cultural activities, diversity workshops, and reentry discussions. To date, the college has witnessed a growth in the international student population, as well as an increasing interest in international programs and the International Studies Co-Major Program.

David C. Prejsnar and Alison Tasch collaborated on the chapter entitled "Mainstreaming International Studies in a Community College," which explores the unique demands of a community college population. The Community College of Philadelphia (CCP) addresses the moral and spiritual challenges of human rights, ecological survival, and community with other cultures and ethnic groups through an approach that "mainstreams" international studies in the community college environment. With their large, nontraditional student body (including more than 2,000 immigrants, some of whom have no previous formal training in English) and limits on resources, CCP had to be creative. Believing that they owed students in the liberal arts an excellent global education, they developed international studies as both a general education requirement and a separate elective course of study. This was accomplished through existing courses and culturally focused mini-majors in international studies. Newer courses, such as the cultural traditions course sequence, were made possible through grants that enable the college to serve a truly global community.

The last chapter, "A Transnational Model for Internationalizing the Curriculum," is written by a faculty member of Waseda University in Japan and by faculty from U.S. institutions affiliated with the university. Michael Mooney, Takehiko Kawase, Michael Reardon, Frederick Nunn, and Ellen Mashiko address the challenge of internationalizing the curriculum at diverse institutions spanning two nations. The project was to design, plan, teach, assess, and administer an intensive, theme-focused, academic summer program which integrates courses, using transcultural and transdisciplinary perspectives, language courses, and shared experiences. But the ability to rethink and shift their approach from bilateral to transnational and theme-focused was essential to the creation of a program that would be equally beneficial to all the institutions and student bodies concerned. For example, this paradigmatic shift influences curricular decisions and thinking at Waseda, Lewis and Clark College, Oregon State University, Pacific University, and Portland State University. The benefits of shared values among students, faculty, and staff have far outweighed difficulties occasioned by differences in organizational structure and operational styles.

In the Appendixes, we have included materials to assist in the development of international studies, including funding opportunities, internship contacts, and a sample syllabus to illustrate how one faculty member approaches the topic of cross-cultural differences.

The goal of this volume is to provide provocative material to encourage institutions to rethink their needs and goals, rather than seeking the perfect design that could be superimposed on an institute of higher learning. We learned from the conference that no matter how different our experiences, we had much to learn from one another. To chart a successful course through our radically transformed world, healthy institutions must be engaged in this debate on the future of international studies in the liberal arts context.

Part I

THE ACADEMY AND INTERNATIONAL STUDIES

Chapter 1

Mustering the Conceptual Resources to Grasp a World in Flux

Tu Wei-ming

Environmentalists sensitive to the issues raised by scholars characterized as deep ecologists, such as Father Thomas Berry, have a troubling perspective on the human condition. The problematique of the viability of the human race, they note, is that having transformed ourselves into the most aggressive and self-destructive animal the evolutionary process has ever witnessed, we have now added ourselves to the long list of endangered species. This is the magnitude of the human dilemma today. We are urgently in need of a new way of perceiving, a new mode of thinking, even a new form of life, which is predicated on a radically transformed attitude and world view.

Paradoxically, our determined effort to move away from militarism, materialism, aggression, conflict, and destruction may be a new discovery, but it is also a return to the spiritual roots that have provided the ground for humans to survive and flourish for centuries. In this sense, our humanity is at a crossroads. But our rational understanding of the predicament and our rhetoric, especially at liberal arts colleges, is so alienated from the realities of life that the ability to find solutions and put them into practice now becomes the real challenge. Once aware of this situation, we become willing to confront the unknown, and begin to sense not only the importance, but the necessity of returning to broadly defined spiritual roots, which ought to be our home.

EMERGENCE OF THE SO-CALLED GLOBAL VILLAGE

I recently spent time with students at Brooklyn High and Cambridge Rindge and Latin School, both in the Boston area, discussing ethical issues. Public high school students are aware that the emergence of the global village demands we explore what may be called core values underlying our shared community and humanity. Sadly, this community is still very much imagined. Ironically, the rise of modern civilization informed by the modern West has so undermined the sense of community implicit in the Hellenistic idea of the citizen, the Judaic idea of the covenant, and the Christian ideal of fellowship, that what the global village symbolizes in reality is difference, differentiation, and discrimination.

The world has never been so divided in power, wealth, and access to information. For example, recently an official of AT&T remarked that more than 50 percent of the human race has never used the telephone, nor are they aware of the telephone; whereas a small fraction of us are now internationally wired on a daily basis. So in our highly fragmented lifeboat, the planet Earth, the authentic possibilities for communication, cooperation, and integration have hardly been realized.

I had a very interesting encounter at Berkeley in the 1970s. While reading about a group of self-described "lifeboat philosophers," who gathered in Santa Barbara to reflect on seminal issues, I immediately had an image of a lifeboat on the open sea, much as an astronaut in space. I made a point to meet the group, and when I shared this image with them, they were stunned, "The Earth! No way! We're talking about Santa Barbara." What they had in mind were various strategies to preserve Santa Barbara as a livable community. They knew it was unconstitutional to not allow others to move into the area, even if it is unspoiled and beautiful, but legally they could control the water supply. These citizens were trying to devise all kinds of ingenious, philosophically sound, and legally practicable measures to defend this particular locale against the outside world.

Thankfully, the inheritors of the great Western traditions, which have maintained highly complex and tension-ridden relationships with the ideology of the modern West, have opened the door for criticism of the anthropocentrism, including the evolution of materialistic progress and aggressive development inherent in the Enlightenment "project." In fact, some of the major universities have been home to much of this criticism. We also hear a lot of arguments against the Enlightenment mentality, superficially understood. True enlightenment is, of course, inner peace and human well-being through cultural interchange, and humane education for the sake of communal self-realization.

UNREALIZED HOPE OF THE EAST

Various life orientations in East Asia as informed by, for example, Mahayana Buddhism, Taoism, Shintoism, and Confucianism, provide sophisticated and even practicable resources in recognizing the sanctity of the Earth, the interconnectedness of all modalities of being, the beneficial interaction between the human community and nature, and the mutuality between heaven and humankind. Some very rich conceptual apparatuses have enabled East Asian thinkers to transcend such exclusive dichotomies as matter/spirit, body/mind, subject/object, sacred/profane, man/nature, and even creator/creature. This ability to transcend may have helped them develop what we have now witnessed in comparative developmental strategies as a modern civilization that is less adversarial, individualistic, and self-interested . Unfortunately, industrial East Asia, Japan and the so-called Four Mini-Dragons (Taiwan, South Korea, Hong Kong, and Singapore) are still far from offering inspiration for the emerging modern global community, because they are enslaved in a thoroughly domesticated, modernistic, instrumental mind set. Instead, these societies exhibit mercantilism, commercialism, materialism, and heartless competitiveness.

Consider the case of Japan. We have been waiting for some kind of cultural message out of Japan, not just karaoke, which literally means "empty orchestra," and not just a communication network. But the process of internationalization, re-Asianization, and indigenization is so complex and sensitive that the creative thinkers in Japan are not able, at least at this juncture, to challenge Fukuzawa Yukichi's powerful thesis of the 1920s that encouraged Japan's withdrawal from Asia to join Europe. For example, in the 1980s Nakasone proudly announced that Japan is part of the West, because it had joined G7, a forum for countries considered to be the world's leading industrial democracies (also including France, the U.S., Britain, Germany, Italy, Canada, and, more recently, Russia and the entity of the European Union). In fact, Japan needs to return home, as defined in global, regional, and local terms. In other words, not only does Japan need to further globalize, it needs to be truthful to its indigenous resources and return to Asia. Because the challenge is so great and the issue so sensitive, a number of thoughtful people in Asia and the West have begun to approach it from the standpoint of what it means to be modern, even the meaning of traditions within modernity, and how the modernizing process may assume different cultural forms.

WHAT IS MODERN?

In the early 1960s, an important sociologist and teacher of mine, by the name of Talcott Parsons, defined modernity in terms of three inseparable dimensions: market economy, democratic polity, and individualism. The collapse of socialism gives the impression that market rather than planned economy, democratic rather than authoritarian polity, and individualist rather than a collectivistic style of life symbolize the wave of the future. The end of history has been described as a stage of human development dominated by only advanced capitalism, characterized by multinational corporations, information superhighways, technology-driven sciences, mass communication, and conspicuous consumption. But regardless of whether we have reached this historic end, we must be critically aware of the globalizing forces that have transformed the world through a variety of networks into a kind of wired discourse community. As a result, distance, no matter how great, does not inhibit communication, and, ironically, territorial proximity does not guarantee contact.

In a recent meeting in Taipei, a friend, Professor Hsü Cho-yün of the University of Pittsburgh, said to me, "Since we can have instant communication with people thousands of miles away, we no longer feel the need to sit down and meet our neighbors." Thus we can be frequent conversation partners with associates thousands of miles away, and strangers to our colleagues and relatives. In a curious way, the world, which has been compressed into an interconnected, ecological, financial, commercial, and electronic system, has never been so divided in wealth, influence, and power.

The imagined or even anticipated global communal village is hardly a cause for celebration. Some people from New York travel all over the world, but others never cross the Brooklyn Bridge to Manhattan. The rich, dominant, articulate, included, informed, and connected are the beneficiaries of the system. They form numerous transnational networks, making distance, and, indeed, ethnic boundaries, cultural diversity, religious exclusivism, or national sovereignty inconsequential in the march toward modernity. In fact, many of the postmodernists have informed us that boundary crossing, along with the continuous, restless, redefining of boundaries, and the ideal of the self, nation, or community have been deconstructed; if we try to essentialize any of them, we are merely modern and not postmodern. But if we focus our attention on some of the very powerful so-called macrotrends that have exerted a shaping influence on the global community since the end of the Second World War—science, technology, communication, trade, finance, entertainment, travel, tourism, migration, and, of course, disease—we may be misled into believing that the human condition itself has been structured by these newly emerging global forces without any reference to our inherited historical and cultural practices.

GLOBALIZATION WITH LOCALIZATION

One of the most significant end-of-the-twentieth-century reflections is the acknowledgment that globalization does not mean homogenization. Most people have given up the idea that modernization tends to overcome difference; rather it intensifies *as well as* lessens ethnic, social, cultural, and religious conflicts. The emergence of primordial ties, such as ethnicity, language, gender, land, class, and faith, as powerful forces in constructing internally defensive cultural identities and externally aggressive religious exclusivities, compels all practical-minded global thinkers to develop new conceptual resources to understand the condition or spirit of our times. Nowadays we are confronted with two conflicting and even contradictory forces in the global community: internationalization or globalization, and localization or communization. As a good example, the United Nations, which came into existence because of the spirit of globalization, must now deal with issues of rootedness and the problems of ethnicity, language, gender, land, class, and faith.

The modernists in the 1960s, and as late as the 1970s, believed these primordial ties are the issues of developing countries, not of highly industrialized ones. In the last fifteen years, we have come to realize that ethnicity in the United States, language in Canada and Belgium, the problem of land and sovereignty all over the world, gender issues, and the question of religious fundamentalism, have been seriously threatening the cohesiveness of highly industrialized societies in the First World. Students of religion who were once concerned about interreligious conflict have become increasingly aware of intrareligious conflict. A religious community with a progressive or radical faction and a conservative or orthodox faction can experience conflict unimaginable in the past.

The resiliency and explosive power of human-relatedness seems to suggest that the great character of the Enlightenment, with its values of instrumental rationality, individual liberty, calculated self-interest, material progress, and rights consciousness, will have to be challenged in a healthy way or reconfigured by some other values. Two examples are an ethic mindful of the need for reasonableness, not abstract instrumental rationality, but reasonableness in any form of negotiation; and descriptive justice, not simply individual liberty. The noted Harvard philosopher, Jack Rawls, has made a major contribution to the theory of justice, but his commitment challenges a deep-rooted American political strength by always putting liberty above equality. So the question of distributive justice is very important. The question of sympathy and empathy also emerges as a central issue in political discourse. In my undergraduate course on Confucian ethics, we raise the question: Which is more essential for moral reasoning, rationality, or sympathy and empathy? We know that a psychopath can be very rational in negotiating a particular path of escape, but one quality he lacks is sympathy for others. He has not lost his instrumental rationality. The question is one of civility, duty consciousness, and responsibility, in addition to rights consciousness. The idea of the dignity of the person is not necessarily predicated on the person as an isolated island or individual, but also on a person as a stream which flows and meets other streams. If we acknowledge our intrinsic worth, how can we afford to have a society in which only self-reliance, not self-cultivation, is an integral part of the educational process? If we put this question in the context of globalization, we do not have a choice. It is not an either/or, but a both/and situation.

CALL FOR A PUBLIC INTELLECTUAL

The need for a new perspective on the human condition seems to be an important concern of virtually all liberal arts colleges, which are better equipped to deal with the problem than professional schools. We know that professionalization, or even rationalization, is a defining characteristic of modernization. But as Max Weber understood it, rationalization is an empowering process that can develop a blindness extremely detrimental to not only individual human self-realization, but to the well-being of society. Whether you look at these issues from the short- or long-term perspective, or with a focused or more diffuse but comprehensive organic one makes a significant difference. Weber, for example, believed that in the modern period, there are only two kinds of intellectuals that will emerge with what he referred to as a "calling." One has politics as a calling, the other, science. I characterize these as the hot and cold approaches. You either involve yourself in politics or detach yourself and cultivate a disinterested spirit in the pursuit of knowledge. Thus you become either a politician or a professor. But we know this dichotomy is too restrictive. What we need is the emergence of a public intellectual.

The public intellectual is someone politically concerned, socially engaged, and culturally sensitive and informed. A person may be a professional, well trained in some specific area of expertise, but this does not make him or her an intellectual. In fact, the vast majority of scholars in major research universities refuse to become intellectuals. They are great scholars, very much in tune with their research agenda, but they are not politically concerned or socially engaged, sometimes even unmindful of the public issues of their day. Max Weber made a very interesting observation: that disenchantment followed the loss of the magic garden, the old period in which people were linked to a kind of organic unity, forever lost. In the modern world, people can rationalize, become professionalized. There is no need for us to be musical to magic or spiritual ideals. Concerning religious matters, Weber acknowledged he was totally unmusical, yet he was obsessed with the question of religion. That is why he developed his sophisticated analysis of the protestant ethic and the spirit of capitalism. Today, to be religiously unmusical is alright, because religion is simply a private matter. This describes a mind set informed by instrumental rationality and not at all by what we desperately need—the kind of cultural sensitivity and competence required to be a public intellectual.

To combat this mind set, we want to make sure that the public intellectual emerges in many spheres of interest in our society. Certainly, some people in the intellectual community continue to play this role, but many of the more powerful and influential individuals are concentrated in the mass media. It is a sign of self-awareness when the mass media calls for the emergence of a public press. But there also must be people in government, the business community, and all kinds of civic communities, including religious organizations, that are committed to transforming the world. The breadth of the need points to the liberal arts colleges as best equipped to train future leaders, not only for the academic community, but as public intellectuals. Increasingly, the overwhelming majority of brilliant graduates of liberal arts colleges and universities are not interested in a career in pure research or scholarship, though many of them will become professionals. Hopefully, they will not be so professionalized as to become insensitive to the role of the public intellectual. Liberal arts colleges must continue to provide the resources that research universities have abandoned to overprofessionalization for the cultivation of the public intellectual. Indeed, liberal arts colleges will provide leaders not just for the academic community, but also the mass media, government, business, civic organizations, religious organizations, and social movements, including environmentalism, feminism, religious pluralism, human rights, and philanthropy for the poor and underprivileged.

LIBERAL ARTS UNDER SIEGE

With liberal arts colleges needed to play this critical role, one trend today places us in a particularly precarious position: the humanities, the core of the liberal arts agenda, are being marginalized. Due to financial constraints, many liberal arts colleges have deliberately turned into institutes of business administration and professional training, with particular emphasis on specific skills, because "it is unaffordable," "not linked to the market," or many of the programs are not considered viable in this tense, competitive market. But in terms of the long perspective, with the whole question of globalization and localization as the background, the humanities are absolutely necessary for human self-understanding and self-reflexivity, both individually and communally. The disciplines in the humanities are language, literature, classics, history, philosophy, and religion. Language or linguistics help us understand not only the tool used to try to communicate, but also self-description, self-identity, and self-understanding. Literature assists our comprehension of the most refined, symbolic manifestation of our inner dreams. History provides an understanding of ourselves in terms of collective memory. Classics help us appreciate our traditions, while philosophy helps examine our thinking, to reflect upon reflections of the various kinds of humanistic projects. Religion aids in understanding our ultimate concerns. If these are marginalized, we are going to fulfill the statement made by the chancellor of the University of California, Clark Kirk, that the primary purpose of higher education is social service, narrowly defined.

In the 1960s, there was a major debate concerning the aims of higher education. Scholars in the humanities and the social and basic sciences argued very forcefully that institutes of higher learning ought to be arenas where cultural transmission is possible, so the basic research and knowledge, especially wisdom, would be passed from generation to generation, independent of the market forces and not dependent upon a narrowly defined social utility. Congress is the worst place for the highest-priority values of society to be negotiated and debated, because it reflects a highly localized, short-term interest that is part of our political culture. Therefore, the universities and colleges ought to be able to serve this important function of cultural transmission. The United States is one of the very few industrialized societies that does not have major, nationally organized institutes in the social sciences and humanities. Japan, France, Germany, Russia, and the People's Republic of China have national institutes of social sciences and humanities, with huge funds devoted to these purposes.

Many radical thinkers in the 1960s also argued, quite forcefully, that institutes of higher learning should provide an opportunity for people to realize themselves in a highly individualistic sense; to allow their talents to flourish without any preconceived model of utility or pragmatism. There is an old Chinese saying: "If you plant a tree, it requires ten years to mature, but if you want to cultivate a talent, one century is needed." Three generations of concerted effort are needed to train human talents. If we do not invest, we will suffer. Finally, we know that institutes of higher learning should also be places where the critical spirit, not just political but social and cultural criticism, will be supported to provide a forum for this kind of self-reflection.

EAST ASIA IN FLUX

If you examine the global situation, the argument to make the liberal arts college the place for training the public intellectual becomes compelling. Consider the rise of East Asia, both industrial East Asia (which includes Japan and the Four Mini-Dragons) and socialist East Asia (which includes mainland China, North Korea, and Vietnam). This is normally characterized as the Confucian area, but in fact the overlaps of religions are significant. We know that in Japan, Shintoism and Mahayana Buddhism are important. In Korea, South Korea in particular, not just Mahayana Buddhism and Shamanism, but increasingly Christianity, are important; 30 percent of Koreans are Christians. And in Taiwan, 2 to 3 percent are Christians, but a higher percentage are Buddhists and Taoists. In mainland China, the religious situation is very fluid. According to one account, China has about 40 million Christians, while another states there are 60 to 80 million. But with a population of 1.2 billion, the percentage is still small. There are Buddhists and Taoists and all kinds of folk religious traditions. And yet East Asia, both industrial and socialist, can still be characterized as Confucian in terms of basic values or life orientation. Professor Reischauer, former American ambassador to Japan, a major scholar and public intellectual in East Asian studies, once remarked that among the Japanese, 80 percent are Shintoists, 85 percent call themselves Buddhists, and yet none deny they are also Confucians.

Since the Second World War, this particular area, first industrial East Asia, now perhaps socialist East Asia, has become the fastest growing region of the world, unprecedented in human history. This is why we hear so much talk about the Pacific Rim. Just two examples: In 1978, United States trade across the Pacific Ocean surpassed the trade across the Atlantic. Thus, in terms of international trade, the Pacific region became even more important than the common market in Europe. In 1996, it is probably approaching twice what it was in 1978. In 1984, the United States went from being the largest creditor country in the world to the largest debtor. With the exception of unified Germany, all the other countries that have contributed to this international trade deficit—Japan, South Korea, Taiwan, and increasingly China—are in Asia. If we look at the Chinese case (it has to be impressionistically, because we have no hard data and the figures are subject to different interpretations), we find that in 1990, the unfavorable balance of payments between United States and China was about $10 billion, and in 1991, $13 billion. Most scholars believed we had reached the plateau. But in 1992, it rose to $18 billion; in 1993, it was over $20 billion; in 1994, $26 billion; and in 1995, over $30 billion. And Japan is at about $46 billion. China is catching up extremely fast. The rise of industrial East Asia has far-reaching implications for the United States in terms of economic competitiveness, political organization, social structure, and cultural values.

BRANDS OF CAPITALISM

Let us reexamine what Talcott Parsons defined as the three inseparable dimensions of modernity, starting with market economy. There is no question that this is a defining characteristic of being modern. No society can afford not to have the market mechanism at work. But even the World Bank now recognizes that the economic development in the Pacific Rim is not due to the market economy alone, the market mechanism per se, but the leadership of the government as well. So we have in this area many different models, not only of government intervention, but leadership. In Japan, it is MITI, the government-sponsored international trade and industry organization that has coordinated virtually all the major international competition for quite some time. In Singapore, the government is directly involved with the private sector by forming government private major corporations. The government in Taiwan visibly encourages middle and small industries and is responsible for gathering information and developing overall strategies. South Korean government identified some of the emerging major multinational corporations and developed them. Hong Kong, characterized as a purely market economy, has been used by Milton Friedman to show that laissez-faire policy really works. But the more we understand Hong Kong, the more we feel this characterization is incorrect. Forty percent of Hong Kong residents actually live in government-built houses. How laissez-faire could that be? In fact, the government is involved in every aspect of the market. So the Hong Kong government, together with the Chinese elite, have now coined an expression called "positive noninterference," with emphasis on the positive.

Democracy is a process, not a static polity. It is rooted in different traditions. British democracy is different from French, which is different from German, which is different from American. The importance of tradition and the gradual transformation of the polity in England provides a stark contrast with the revolutionary spirit and anticlericalism of the French experience. German democracy is not unrelated to nationalism and the need to catch up to France and England. Democracy in the United States is rooted in the vibrancy of civil society. There are different forms of democratic structures, but can there be a Japanese, Taiwanese, Hong Kong, or People's Republic of China form of democracy? The most intriguing question is really that of individualism. Talcott Parsons believed that individualism was so much a part of the modernizing process that he could not imagine modernization without it. But as East Asia appears to show, human relatedness and networking is just as important. In fact, many scholars like Gary Hamilton of the University of Washington, Seattle, have characterized capitalist formation in East Asia as network capitalism, different from the kind that has emerged in the West.

This means we have to think in terms of traditions within modernity, and that the modernizing process has already assumed different cultural forms. Certainly there is the Western European form, the North American form, and obviously now there is an East Asian form. Will there be an Islamic, Hindu, South Asian, or African form? We need to think about these possibilities, as well as our own strengths and limitations. The strength of East Asian society is really twofold. East Asian intellectuals, public intellectuals in particular, have been devoted students of Western learning for more than a century, or at least three generations. They first were students of Dutch learning—what the Japanese call "Rangaku"—then they pursued English, French, and German learning, and in the last 40 years, American learning. Thus, an intellectual in East Asia is someone seasoned in the knowledge of the West; to know English, French, or German is a requirement. They managed to tap their indigenous resources *and* the various advanced ideologies and technologies of the West to make the intellectual community in East Asia vibrant. Even in purely social Darwinian terms, they are quite competitive. It is therefore necessary that American public intellectuals trained in liberal arts colleges and universities be able to respond to the East Asian challenge creatively, imaginatively, and effectively. At a minimum, this means moving away from monolinguism. The joke is that if you know two languages you are bilingual, if you know multiple languages you are multilingual, and if you know one language you are American. The belief that English will eventually be spoken by everyone and that it is a waste to invest time to study foreign languages is not only self-defeating, but also extremely detrimental even in a purely economic sense, not to mention the capacity to understand other cultures.

TOWARDS A GLOBAL DIALOGUE

The need for the dialogue of civilization, not what Samuel Huntington calls "the clash of civilization," is to recognize an obvious fact which Huntington would have us ignore in his explanatory model of "the West and the rest." His model, defined in terms of geopolitical power relations, is predicated on the belief that North America and Western Europe will form one cultural unit, and it will need Japan as a junior partner, even though Japan seems to represent an alien culture. According to the model, it is also necessary and desirable to cultivate good relations with Latin American countries, Russia, and Eastern European countries, because they are Catholic and Eastern Orthodox and thus share the same religious vocabulary. Ignore South Asia, India, and Africa, because they are not a threat, at least not in the next 20 or 30 years. Be wary of two cultures: Confucian culture in East Asia—China in particular, but also North Korea and Vietnam—and the Islamic world, both in the Middle East and Asia.

We know intellectually this is not very sophisticated, and culturally and religiously it is probably wrong; yet this scenario is very powerful. In fact, it is so powerful that the mass media and the government, whether by default or conscious design, react to the international scene based on this scenario. We know it is intellectually indefensible, because if you come up with an intellectual map of the world, one great spiritual tradition is not even mentioned: Buddhism. Why? Because Buddhism cannot be geopolitically specific. Buddhism is in Boston, as well as Latin America and Southeast Asia. But this is also true of Christianity. How can you say that a Bostonian Christian is more Christian than, say, a Korean Christian in Seoul? Theologically and intellectually you cannot make that claim. You cannot say that a Buddhist in Japan is more Buddhist than one in San Francisco. We know that Islam constitutes the second largest religion in the United States. There are more Muslims than Jews. There are more Muslims in Paris than Protestants, although most Parisians are Catholics. The religious situation is extremely fluid.

The chair of the Committee on the Study of Religion at Harvard, Professor Diana Eck, has been engaged in a project on religious pluralism in Boston. She is trying to understand the religious landscape. The diversity of religions, not to mention the new religions, is incredible. To somehow imagine that the Christian world is against the Confucian or Islamic world and in agreement with others, is very difficult to defend and may even turn out to be disastrous for the imperative "dialogue" among religious groups. Indeed, the West is in the rest, because westernization is going on all over the world. But the rest is also now in the West. We need to become more self-reflective about understanding the changing landscape of the international scene, because the globalizing process is being duplicated in our own local environment almost on a daily basis. The largest concentration of Koreans outside of the capital city of Seoul turns out to be in Los Angeles. Los Angeles also has the largest concentration of Thai outside of Bangkok. Today we are seeing the second migration of Chinese. These affluent Chinese are different from the first migrants in the nineteenth century, who came from Hong Kong, Taiwan, Malaysia, and Indonesia and went to Australia, New Zealand, and Canada. For example, in Vancouver, 40 percent or more of the residents are Chinese, largely from Hong Kong. Now you have a second migration, and the situation is very fluid. It is important to think about what spiritual resources we can mobilize to help us think thorough this incredible predicament. We have to be ecumenical, we have to be inclusive. We need to understand the situation based on our own cultural tradition—Greek philosophy, Roman law, Judaism, and Christianity. But we also must take into account non-Western traditions such as Islam, Hinduism, Jainism, Confucianism, Taoism, Buddhism, and various kinds of indigenous traditions, such as Native American, Hawaiian, Maori, African tribal, and Inuit.

Finally, perhaps more important is to train our public intellectuals at liberal arts universities and colleges to understand the powerful self-awareness within the modern West emerging in the past few years with the environmentalists, feminists, religious pluralists, and communitarian ethicists. These are new trends that cannot be easily understood, either by the mass media, the government or other important players in the public realm. They are certainly not well understood by research universities because of their structural limitations, but the liberal arts colleges are strategically positioned to understand these trends.

In conclusion, I offer a personal reflection on a new ethic or life orientation informed by a moral vision. This new ethic requires the formulation of what we might call ethical intelligence that is responsive to our times. Research universities and others are well equipped to transmit knowledge, information, and cognitive and rational intelligence, but not ethical intelligence. My conception of ethical intelligence is predicated on the Confucian faith in the improvability of the human condition.

A few years ago, I was asked to write a short statement on the meaning of life for *Life Magazine.* I was informed that the magazine had also asked the Pope and the Dalai Lama. I was flattered. I told myself, this is a serious enterprise. When it was published, the Dalai Lama did have a statement, but the Pope did not respond. Yet, Oliver North, a cab driver from Boston, and Nixon responded. Altogether, 50 responses were published. My statement reads:

Copernicus decentered the earth. Charles Darwin relativized the godlike image of man. Karl Marx exploded the idea of social harmony, and Sigmund Freud complicated our conscious life. They have redefined humanity for the modern age, yet they have also empowered us with a communal, critical self-awareness to renew our faith in the ancient Confucian wisdom that the globe is the center of our universe and the only hope for us, and that the Mandate of Heaven enjoins us to make our bodies healthy, our hearts sensitive, our minds alert, our souls refined, and our spirits brilliant. We are here because embedded in our human nature is the secret code for Heaven's self-realization. Heaven is certainly omnipresent, may even be omniscient, but it is most likely not omnipotent. It needs our active participation to realize its own truth. We are Heaven's partners, indeed co-creators. We serve Heaven with our common sense, the lack of which nowadays has brought us to the brink of self-destruction. Since we help Heaven to realize itself through our self-discovery and self-understanding in day-to-day living, the ultimate meaning of life is found in our ordinary human existence.

Chapter 2

The Liberal Arts Role: Cultivating a Common Ethic of Care

Peter S. Thacher

Forty-eight years ago, two friends were about to begin their junior year abroad at the Sorbonne, sponsored by Sweet Briar College. We had all been in college at home under the GI Bill, but now we were in Paris, and they came to me because I was the only American they knew there who had a job. By the vagaries of service in the war, I had graduated that spring and just started working with the Marshall Plan; they were enrolled at the Sorbonne, but faced one last obstacle: they needed a signed affidavit certifying that each was, "of sufficient emotional maturity so as successfully to withstand the temptations of a foreign culture." Feeling scholarly in a bistro late that night, we admired the careful avoidance of a split infinitive in a statement we otherwise found absurd. But the wine overcame my scruples, and I signed it.

We've come a long way since then, and I commend the leadership shown by those schools that are helping to expose succeeding generations of students to better knowledge of a world full of cultural temptations and diversity. These institutions recognize that an interdependent global society is taking shape, in which their students can have meaningful roles to play. That makes these schools unique, a very small but influential group on whose work future stability and well-being may largely depend.

For outside of this effort, there are far more visible, newsworthy events that show dangerous drifts into chaos: intercommunal strife, genocide, refugees, a breakdown of the fabric of society. In recent years, our attention has been drawn to Somalia, Haiti, Rwanda, Cambodia, Burundi, Yugoslavia, Israel; now we have a murderous attack in Manchester, England, and precarious politics in Russia. Which is the dominant trend in a world freed of Cold War tensions and cohesion? Can rational ways be found to manage on a disorderly, crowded planet?

Let me provide some examples from my experience to explain why the future of international studies programs is so vitally important. Before becoming an international civil servant, I had served on various U.S. negotiating teams addressing arms control issues. One of these was the Partial Test Ban Treaty of 1963; it could also be seen as the first global environmental treaty. This was not just a "feel-good" treaty of good intentions. By 1980, there was a measurable decline of radiation doses caused by nuclear weapons testing, from about 7 percent of natural background radiation in the early 1960s, to less than 1 percent. Nor was it a one-time quick-fix; negotiations underway in June of 1996 in Geneva will hopefully produce a complete ban on all nuclear weapons tests by the end of the year, 33 years later. And all of this started at the height of the Cold War.

Concern over our common destiny can overcome the divisions among us if we really try to understand each other—that is the job for the educators—and think about the future.

As an international civil servant on Maurice Strong's staff preparing the Stockholm Conference, I was responsible for pollutants of international significance, and the institutional arrangements we would recommend to governments. One issue we focused on in 1971 was the threat to stratospheric ozone posed by the prospect of a second generation of commercial supersonic transport (SST) planes that would fly slightly higher, in the lower reaches of the stratosphere, where jet emissions could destroy ozone at those altitudes. For economic as well as environmental reasons, second-generation SSTs were never built.

Nonetheless, at the first meeting of the United Nations Environment Program's (UNEP) Governing Council in 1973, Maurice Strong proposed a new budget line for our program called "Outer Limits":

The environmental dialogue and the attendant discussion of various "Doomsday" scenarios imply the existence of certain "Outer Limits" to changes which man's activities may engender in some elements of the biosphere. If exceeded, these may endanger the continuance of human life on this planet. For example, possible outer limits have been pointed to in relation to the generation of heat, the carbon dioxide content of the atmosphere, the ozone content of the stratosphere, and the health of the oceans.

One year later, the first speculative article by Sherry Rowland and Mario Molino appeared in *Nature*, for which, with Paul Crutzen, they were to win the Nobel Prize in 1995. The resulting attention triggered by this 1974 paper lent a new urgency to UNEP's work with the World Meteorological Organization, the International Council of Scientific Unions, and many other UN system agencies. UNEP was involved in a working group on stratospheric and mesospheric problems that produced a state-of-the-art review in 1976 and then focused on monitoring total ozone and its vertical distribution, and the determination of long-term exposure to ultraviolet radiation.   Work was underway outside the UN system as well; the Organization for Economic Cooperation and Development (OECD) Environment Committee was collecting data from the private sector on the production and use of fluorocarbons in the OECD countries; UNEP requested similar data from non-OECD countries.

By 1976, our governing council agreed on the need for "a meeting of appropriate international, governmental, and nongovernmental organizations to review all aspects of the ozone layer, identify related ongoing activities and future plans, and agree on a division of labor and a coordinating mechanism for, inter alia, the compilation of research activities and future plans, and the collection of related industrial and commercial information."

At the resulting meeting in Washington in March 1977, a "World Plan of Action on the Ozone Layer" was adopted, setting forth 21 sets of far-reaching actions to examine the natural state of the ozone layer and its modification by human actions, the impacts of change on man and ecosystems, and socioeconomic aspects.

One of these recommendations in the monitoring category was critical for what would follow; it called for the reactivation of the total-ozone station at Halley Bay, the U.K. station in Antarctica, to continue collecting background data on overhead ozone. A shortage of science funding in London had threatened to close expensive facilities in Antarctica since the International Geophysical Year in the late 1950s, specifically including a Dobson ozone spectrophotometer measuring total overhead ozone. Armed with what amounted to an international seal of approval, British funds were found to reactivate this instrument which would, many years later, allow Dr. Joseph Farmer to discover the existence of a phenomena that exceeded everyone's speculation; so much so that publication of the findings were delayed a year in order to double-check the data.

Indeed, even the overhead satellite readings from NIMBUS 7 were initially rejected as probable instrument failures, until Farmer's data triggered their analysis; this was how the existence of the "Antarctic Hole" was confirmed.

From there on, it was history. While the significance of the Antarctic Hole was not fully appreciated until 1988, scientific and public concerns aroused by it drove the process that led to signature of the Montreal Protocol in September 1987. Since then, with leadership by Dupont and other manufacturers, that treaty has been tightened further and amended to speed the cutoff of production of harmful substances, and international funding has been mobilized to assist developing countries in contributing to the common good.

Early indications of success from these agreements was reported last year, when it was found that although chlorine levels continued to increase in the stratosphere, their rate of increase was falling. This year, levels of chlorofluorocarbons (CFCs) in the troposphere closer to the ground have been found to be lower than before. Here again, it was not just a "feel-good" agreement, but part of an ongoing process that started a quarter century ago by which diverse information is continually integrated through international cooperation among a wide variety of governmental and nongovernmental bodies and disciplines, with a vital role played by the private sector.

But it is too early to be confident. J. C. Farmer, former director of the British Antarctic Survey, whose Dobson instrument first announced the phenomena of the Antarctic Hole, cautioned in a letter published in the *Washington Post*, that bromine and other ozone-depleting substances continue to load the atmosphere, and that colder Arctic winters in the stratosphere may speed ozone destruction. "It is 11 years since my team first reported Antarctic ozone depletion, and it is too soon for complacency," Farmer wrote.

Now that we recognize human impacts are measurable at local, regional, and global scales, the challenge is to cope with man-made contributions to global change, not only by international research and monitoring programs to improve our understanding and ability to predict anthropogenic impacts, but, more daunting, to take account of that knowledge to reorder human actions (and inactions) so as to reduce risk of harmful impacts—at all scales—while improving socioeconomic conditions on a crowded planet, and ensuring that resources needed in the future are not needlessly used up now.

At the "Earth Summit" in Rio in 1992, governments agreed on "Agenda 21," an action plan to achieve sustainable development, and on a number of formal agreements—such as the treaties on climate change and biodiversity—as well as declarations of principles. But even with complete understanding, the diverse value systems that shape decision making here and abroad strain one's confidence that an effective approach can be found during the coming decades when, once again, as in my lifetime, the global population will double, and existing resources will be exploited to meet growing demands.

True, the Partial Test Ban Treaty and Montreal Protocol show that even at a global scale agreements can be reached to curb human actions that otherwise contribute to global change in ways threatening life on this planet. In the first case, we came to agree that harm had been done and should be reduced. In the ozone agreement, we agreed *before* harm had been recognized and decided to take *preventive* action, the first time ever. Neither could have been tackled without multidisciplinary approaches at the international level, integrating information and specialists from diverse fields, not limited to the natural sciences, but increasingly drawing on the social sciences as well, to come to grips with human factors that alter natural systems and cycles.

But in both the test ban and stratospheric/ozone issues, it was the "haves" that were the primary cause of the problem, and they bore most of the burden of effective action. Significant efforts are underway to find ways to deal *preventively* with risks looming in the "have-nots," but it is obviously easier to get agreement among the rich than among the poor. Climate change and related energy problems are far more complex and will need new efforts by the "haves" to influence new decision makers abroad.

In one of her many insightful statements, Connecticut College President Claire Gaudiani challenged an audience "to imagine that the 'haves' will come to believe that their first priority, if they and their children are to remain well-off in the long term, is to ensure that the poor grow better off each year" (Gaudiani 1995, 11).

Climate change compels us to face this. Current energy-per-capita figures are already tragically insufficient to meet the needs of most of the world's population, yet even with no improvement in their condition, sheer demographic growth alone in the so-called developing countries, may increase the CO_2 levels and heat "our" planet to dangerous levels. In effect, even if Americans improve our use of energy to produce goods and services to the level of France, with an economy that is twice as energy efficient as ours, and we significantly reduce our greenhouse contributions—as required under the Climate Convention—China (now the number two in greenhouse gas emissions) and other coal-dependent countries will continue to heat our common greenhouse, possibly exceeding "outer limits." It will be very much in our best interests as "haves" to ensure that China and other "have-nots" enjoy energy-efficient technologies no less effective than our own.

Of course, it will take the combined work of many professions and specialists to cope with these issues, but, above all, it will call for American leadership by generalists working in a variety of fields at the international level to tip the scales in favor of a rational approach for the common good, amid many continuing tendencies towards chaos and simplistic assumptions.

The earlier emphasis on natural science research and monitoring programs has laid a good basis of broader understanding that now requires application of a wide range of socioeconomic skills and insights to reduce poverty and other inequities in a world where the gap between haves and have-nots is increasing rapidly, at all scales—from local to global—and to do this in a way that achieves both environmental and economic objectives.

The role of American international studies programs is absolutely vital in shaping the outlook of future leaders. Many countries will continue to make important contributions, as they have in the eradication of smallpox, the operation of a World Weather Watch that underpins the TV forecasts we take for granted here, and the many other success stories, two of which I outlined. But all of these were made possible in large part because of initiatives and institutional and human resources which were mobilized here in the United States.

U.S. influence and leadership at the international level will continue to be critical, and international studies programs can play a major role in strengthening it. But, as Julia Kushigian, director of the Toor Cummings Center at Connecticut College commented, governance is evolving in this interdependent world. Secretary of State Christopher recently pronounced that U.S. national interests, including security, are put at risk by environmental degradation abroad and that these issues will therefore receive more attention in U.S. foreign policy.

But this does not mean what it might have meant a half century ago, when governments could set up the United Nations on behalf of "we the people" it was to represent, and when Americans were still determined to "withstand the temptations of a foreign culture." Governments are no longer in charge to the degree they were, and new groups, identified as major actors in Rio's Agenda 21, have increasing influence over the future. These include scientists and engineers, mayors and governors, women, youth, farmers, business people, parliamentarians, indigenous peoples, and, of course, environmentalists.

Even more than well-trained foreign service officers representing governments, we need knowledgeable citizens in all walks of life whose conduct, whether as journalists, scientists, entrepreneurs, or agitators, can help encourage a common ethic of care for the well-being of the planet and its resources, including its people. This calls for a redoubling of efforts within the liberal arts context and far greater effort to overcome shortcomings in the U.S. education system, with earlier attention to world history—not just U.S. history—and languages and geography, and an emphasis on multidisciplinarity at all levels.

Twenty years ago, my wife and I came to Connecticut from Nairobi to start looking at colleges for our children, one of whom was to graduate from Connecticut College in 1982. We made what I thought was an amazing discovery at the library on the college campus which, to this day, I find thrilling and a great source of hope for the future. Having lived in Europe, we recognized the same sort of card file and system for identifying and locating books that we saw here. Anywhere else, the normal procedure is to fill out the form, give it to a clerk, and wait. If you are lucky, the clerk finds it, records it, and gives you the book. Here, however, in college libraries across the land, the normal practice is to go into the stacks yourself and, if you are lucky, you will find the book you are looking for, as well as many other related books of which you had never heard. Open access to the stacks is a uniquely American practice, one that reflects attitudes about freedom of, and access to, information that may be of profound value in the future.

Twenty years ago we did not have the check-out safeguards that are now commonplace in stores and libraries. The president of Connecticut College, Oakes Ames, was an old friend, and when we called on him, I expressed my excitement about our "discovery," but asked if the college didn't lose lots of books with open access to the stacks. He said it was a problem, they were working on it, but he thought it was probably one of the best uses of money available to the college.

This attitude brings me to a recollection from the last speech Adlai Stevenson gave at a UN meeting in Geneva, a few days before his death. His concluding words were, "It all depends on the care and, dare I say it, the love, we give this planet, our Spaceship Earth."

REFERENCE

Gaudiani, Claire L. 1995. "Global Social Development: Higher Education's Next Moral Commitment." *Educational Record* (winter): 11.

Chapter 3

Tossed into a New Frame: Learning before Teaching

Claire L. Gaudiani

In the 50 years before the end of the Cold War, there existed, in the words of one of our presidents, "an evil empire." So life was simple. We knew who the enemy was, who our allies were, and that international studies would be taught essentially within a certain frame of reference. Compared to the post-Cold War world we face today, that world appears almost one-dimensional.

Since the dissolution of the U.S.S.R. and the fall of the Berlin Wall, we are in a completely different ball game with new rules, and colleges must rethink the framework for international studies. Because we were all educated in an earlier game, we are playing in this ball game without knowledge of the rules. Unless we are willing to contemplate an ethical framework in a profoundly different global society, we will manage only to put on a new hat, different stripes and cut our uniform a little more smartly to look chic, but we will not be different, and we must *be* different to teach in this new period. We must start with who we are and what we believe, then ask our colleagues to think about who they are and what they believe, given this new framework. Only then should we tamper with curriculum, let alone the structures that undergird it, such as the programs, centers, fellowships, or internships.

Juan Somavia, Chilean representative to the United Nations, and a number of people who have been working on the set of six United Nations-sponsored global summits taking place since 1990 were, in a sense, prescient in seeing the transformation that was occurring around the world as we moved away from a bipolar and bimodal structure to something extremely more complicated. Those six summits, including one focusing on the child, one on women, one on global social development in Copenhagen, and most recently, one on habitat, were basically guided by the notion that there is an emerging global consensus around some locally appropriate form of democracy that balances individual rights and opportunities with responsibility for the common good. The summits also acknowledged the growing consensus that some form of markets is, for the moment, the optimal economic system. But what we have not developed anywhere is a consensus on an optimal social system.

As teachers and administrators, we guide students into a world where most of the big questions remain problematic. For instance, why are some of the Asian countries doing so well economically in light of a substantial absence of democracy? We need to figure out what this means in terms of our curriculum and how to teach students not to simply be followers of systems, but transformers and creators of more just democracies, economies, and of societies more just and prosperous for all citizens.

Before we think about politics and economics, we must think about human beings. As faculty teaching in the context of the liberal arts, we are connecting with a tradition that is as old as recorded human thought. The tradition of the liberal arts connects us across cultures, around the world, and throughout time to a continuing conversation regarding who we are as human beings. This integration creates a very important aspect to the pursuit of international studies now in this post-Cold War environment. The ethical framework in which one thinks about the political, economic, and social system has to be considered first and then persistently through the rest of the decisions we make, both in society and education. We must talk with colleagues not only about who we are, but what kind of people we have to be in order to be teachers in this new time, and what we need to do to become these people.

The faculty at Connecticut College decided it was willing to put itself in Third World environments—now we say "pursuing roads less traveled"—because it realized that many had not spent time in these areas, unless they had been in the Peace Corps or a similar program. The faculty realized that we live in one frame of reference and were preparing students for a world we do not know ourselves. The framework is so vitally different, because the ethos in which the action and the thinking take place is so different from that of people in former third and second world settings. We need to see these worlds to legitimize our teaching.

Our faculty has gone to Mysore, India, Ghana, Capetown, South Africa, and Puebla, Mexico. Usually, two faculty and between 20 and 30 students go to live in these countries for a semester. They participate in a kind of learning characterized by statements such as, "I don't know what to do about this either," or "I've never done my work in this environment before, but I am going to try to do it." The everyday life is dramatically different from home—the food, the thinking, the coming-to-terms, after all is said and done, with brothers and sisters, with people who teach in their simplicity or in their complexity, or as much as they are willing to share their lives. These are "places I will never forget once I have left there," some faculty members have said.

Our faculty has found in certain settings that students must be allowed to lead, because their flexibility and openness makes them better able to be with people who are different from them. We, who are so well-educated and trained in our thinking and expectations, may miss the very kernel we need to grasp in order to be who we need to be in this unfamiliar setting. We must be willing to change ourselves as, let us say, midcareer people. We must be willing to take ourselves back to the beginning, and say to ourselves, "I will start all over again. I will go to a new place, and I will be like a graduate student again."

We all wish we could go back and start over again, knowing what we know now. In fact, this is the chance; we can start again and examine all the premises and assumptions on which we built our world view, because we know we have built a world view. Whether it is a little left or a little right, democratic or republican, Marxist or free market, it is ours and it is certainly good, because we are over 40, and we know what we are doing.

Maybe we need to get tossed into a frame where everything is different. Maybe as women who *think* we understand feminism, we ought to spend some time with women who understand feminism and come from places with names we cannot pronounce, even though we are in the field of international studies. We need to do this for ourselves, and then provide such opportunities for our colleagues, but we must begin with ourselves. We need to reexamine our own thinking and be willing to put ourselves in vulnerable positions—vulnerable in the sense that our assumptions be thrown into the air and come down in unfamiliar ways, making us have to truly rethink, to truly throw out whole aspects of the syllabus and let new things into our curriculum. But it is not just changing the curriculum or developing the programs, it is starting with ourselves and our colleagues, being well-educated and willing to change first, then to work on the curriculum.

It may well be that the work for students entering the twenty-first century will be focused on developing a social system where everyone can experience some democratic rights and the benefits of a productive market economy. This will be tremendously difficult work. It will create different kinds of allegiances. It will call on people to function in ways unknown in the past; that is, to talk and listen to each other, actually demonstrate deep listening—not just waiting to speak—and demonstrate it by asking follow-up questions. Putting what someone has said inside of what we think, thought, and were going to say, rather than juxtaposing it, is not our usual modus operandi. Our habits as academics are to analyze, criticize, and break things down into component parts. In the coming century, we will need to synthesize. We need to understand fundamentally, as we have been saying on this campus in the context of another project, that democracy is a discussion. As faculty responsible to help our students begin the work of the twenty-first century, we must personally expose ourselves to dramatic changes and live some changes with our students.

We have to rethink our training, not only in terms of its content and how things have changed since we were educated, but how we were taught to speak and reason in an academic context. Is it enough to leave students with the ability to analyze and criticize, and not to create, in the end, synthesis? Is it enough to help them create a hypotheses and prove a position, and not help them find a way to mediate a best solution under the circumstances? It is not enough. It might have been enough in a very neat bipolar, bimodal, Cold War world frame, but that is gone.

The Zapatistas could speak to the world, because they were on-line with CNN. While the Mexican government was saying, "We are not deploying tanks," the powerbook messenger was sending in the coordinates that proved the government wrong. Because the Zapatistas had a powerbook, they were not overwhelmed. The deterioration of their situation and their ability to communicate it to the rest of the world meant that their predicament affected the political situation in Mexico and the rest of us. Not only "us" in this country, but global leaders. It affected us politically and economically. The South American market dropped 39 points in one day, when it became clear that the Mexican government was lying. The potential for social destabilization provoked the threat of political and economic destabilization, and capital flight was the result.

In this instance, our global market framework came alive. We cared so much that $100 million was at stake immediately, and American banks began to feel it. The American President tried to find $40 million to stabilize the peso. He did not succeed, only securing half the amount and having to go hat in hand to Europe and Asia to get the rest.

What was the cause of this near catastrophe? A very unhappy group of indigenous people. Of course, there were other things going on in Mexico, such as a naive government not considering the signals it was sending to the financial market. But a look at what happened between December 1994 and March 1995 shows the effects that one small group of people, ignored by their government, had on not just their own situation or in Mexico or Latin America, but globally. This is important, because it is an illustration that we are all connected, not only by the global market, but to each other's well-being. It was the well-being of the people of Chiapas that was the important factor. Social well-being will be an important focus for the resolution of challenges that our students will face.

A liberal arts education as a fundamental aspect of the work ahead will give students, and all of us as faculty, a renewed chance to reexamine the wisdom of humankind throughout the ages. As we study it in the present, go to places we have never been before, and try to let ourselves be transformed there, we will be able to take and transform education, so that the future will not simply be an extrapolation from what has happened, but the result of what we have chosen—not just with each other, or even with each other and our students, but also with people around the world.

Hopefully, we will be able to truly make common cause, because others will have informed our way of knowing what to want and what to work for.

We all know that Americans still have a disproportionate influence on what happens in the global frame. It is more important than ever in this post-Cold War, complex environment that we be learners and listeners in the global frame before we decide to be educators and transformers. This is very important work, which will make us people about whom someone will look back and say, "They made some very significant changes in higher education at the end of the century in the United States. The thinking that emerged then is the reason why things have developed as they have, and we can enjoy the life we are enjoying now in 2020."

Chapter 4

Synthesis and Tension: Creating an International Studies Program

Robert E. Proctor

As founding director of The Toor Cummings Center for International Studies and the Liberal Arts (CISLA), I was involved in creating the Center at Connecticut College from the inception. Although somewhat autobiographical, the process of creating the Center is relevant, because traveling in my capacity as director and talking with other schools about our program, I found others struggling with some of the same issues.

The idea for the Center came from our president, Claire Gaudiani, who had been the associate director of the Lauder Institute at the Wharton School of Business and Finance at the University of Pennsylvania. Before she was officially inaugurated at Connecticut College in 1988, Dr. Gaudiani had a dinner for all of us who teach a foreign language. She told us about Wharton's program, in which people gain oral proficiency in a foreign language and do a work-study internship abroad as part of the MBA program. Then she posed the question, "Are you willing to try to do something similar at Connecticut College?"

I had just finished writing a book on the history of the humanities. In the process of trying to figure out how to define the humanities and where they came from, my research took me back not only to Renaissance Italy and Petrarch, but beyond Petrarch to Cicero, Petrarch's favorite classical writer. In my own life, I had discovered the liberal arts at their point of origin, in classical antiquity. As I listened to Dr. Gaudiani talk to us at the dinner that night, I thought, "This is great, but too preprofessional for a liberal arts college. How can we have international studies at a liberal arts college? How can we conduct international studies in a liberal arts context? How can we think about the past, as well as the present and the future?"

Since I had tenure and did not worry about being fired, I wrote Dr. Gaudiani that this was a good idea for a graduate school, but we needed to find a way to put this vision in a context of Connecticut College. Her response was a request that we find a way to do this. An *ad hoc* faculty committee met for a whole year and put together the basic intellectual structure of the International Studies Certificate Program, which is part of the Center. I would write to the committee every now and then, reminding them that we needed to talk about tradition as well as modernity. This was sort of my accession over time, never thinking I would end up being director. But when you feel impassioned about something, sooner or later, someone will ask you to do it.

After the committee gave its report, President Gaudiani asked me to be the founding director for the Center. Suddenly I was no longer suggesting to other people what they should do, but figuring out how we were going to put a liberal arts vision within a modern international context. When I look back upon my time as director of CISLA, I see this particular problem as essentially the greatest and most interesting challenge we have faced so far. In part, the support we received from the Henry B. Luce Foundation and others confirmed the importance of talking about the liberal arts.

What do we mean by liberal arts, and how does this fit into an international context? One way of thinking about every college and university in the United States is that each is a unique mix of three conflicting educational traditions. The oldest tradition, which the pilgrims brought over from England and characterized American colonial times, is the liberal arts. This goes back to the humanist schools of the Renaissance and eventually to classical antiquity, a tradition which is essentially theoretical and moral. It says that the goal of learning is to understand reality as a whole, to see all the disciplines as complementary ways of understanding this whole, and the individual as part of it. Built into this tradition is the idea of self-transcendence. In the short speech *Pro Archia*, which Cicero gave in 62 B.C. in defense of his former teacher Archias's Roman citizenship, Cicero provides the first full description of the liberal arts, the *artes liberales*. This very short speech contains all the things we say about liberal arts and is an interesting touchstone to thinking about what we want to do with that tradition today.

The idea of self-transcendence is an important element, and certainly in the Roman context, the speech gives a sense that there comes a moment in each person's life when he must rise above his own concerns and serve the common good. So today, when we talk about the value of leadership or service for the common good, it is part of the liberal arts tradition we inherit. Obviously, in colonial America this tradition was used to prepare a certain group of elite people to assume positions of responsibility, primarily as legislators. But those of us who belong to the liberal arts tradition still have this as part of our own mission, our own calling; we are preparing students not just to get a job, but give back to the world some of what we have given them. So this is the liberal arts tradition that we inherit.

The second tradition, which comes in conflict with the first, evolved in the 1860s when Congress passed the Morrell Act and created land-grant colleges and universities with the express purpose of creating people who would help America industrialize, such as lawyers, engineers, and physicians. This comes in conflict with the liberal arts tradition when a student says to me, "What can I do with a major in Italian literature?" That tradition says the goal of education is to get a job and become employable. At Connecticut College, we feel that tension.

The third tradition is actually one of my alma mater, the Johns Hopkins University, which was created in 1874 with the express purpose of bringing the model of the German research university, the Ph.D.-granting university, to the United States. Johns Hopkins was so successful that other major universities, such as Princeton, Harvard, and Yale, very quickly followed suit. That tradition says the goal of learning is the discovery or creation of knowledge. All of us who have Ph.D.s belong to this tradition, and the tension that it creates with the liberal arts tradition is between specialization and generalization; between general education and doing specific work within your major. It is what Newman might call the enlargement of the mind and the contraction of the mind. This is another tension we live with. The challenge we had in thinking about how to conduct international studies in a liberal arts context was to see whether it was possible to live with these traditions and the tensions among them in a creative synergistic way, while at the same time making the liberal arts tradition the overarching one. Every school will attempt this in its own way. At Connecticut College, we had many struggles as we tried to do it in our own context.

First of all, in creating the Center for International Studies and the Liberal Arts, we made the heart of the Center the International Studies Certificate Program, because our original goal was to internationalize education at the college. This program is not a major, but an attempt to internationalize every major. Students enter the program in the middle of their sophomore year, around the time they are in the process of choosing a major. The message to students and faculty is: Whatever your major, whatever your interests, whether it is art, zoology, or economics, you have an international destiny because of the inherent globalizing tendencies of modernity. The way you can fulfill this is not by majoring in something called international studies, but by finding a way of putting your own major in an international context. For my own thinking, the international context was the liberal arts whole of Cicero and others. It was seeing oneself as part of the global whole. So the first challenge was to find a way we could work together with faculty and students so that students would pursue the major and internationalize it.

The second challenge was to get students to realize that no matter how deeply involved they were in the major, the major had inherent limitations, because no single area of knowledge is totally capable of understanding reality as a whole. The message that we built into the program was: Do your major well, but you also need to show its limitations by putting it in a much broader context. We created three questions for students to reflect upon and answer over the three years in the program. The first is, What are the origins and dynamics of modern global society? This is essentially a sociological question. It has been primarily the sociological tradition that first talked about tradition and modernity, and about the globalizing tendencies inherent in modernity. Not all the faculty agreed with this; they argued that we do not have a modern global society. We asked those students who did not agree to show why it was wrong. Our goal was to find common areas for reflection.

The second question initially was, What are the differences between a traditional and a modern society? However, after two years, we did away with that question, because faculty could not agree on a definition of tradition. We ask instead, What can be gained from a dialogue with the past? The goal is to get students to think more broadly than just about the present. Every historical period has certain challenges. The particular challenge of modernity is overcoming amnesia, since most educators today agree that students either do not have much of a sense of the past or deem it not worthy of consideration. From an artistic, moral, cultural, and ethical point of view, we have much to learn from premodern societies, and some of that knowledge may help us address the challenges of the future. So this is a call for students to think historically.

The third question is, What are some of the material and spiritual challenges of modernity? This question fits with the liberal arts ideal of leadership and addressing issues of the common good. Some of the faculty did not like the word "spiritual." They said it should be "moral" or "ethical." I insisted on keeping "spiritual," because we wanted to cast the net as broadly as possible, and there are many people who believe the challenges are spiritual. I was happy that we left this word in, because several people actually came to the Center planning to address spiritual issues, which we had left somewhat undefined.

Students in the Center have to address the three questions in three papers as part of the initial course during their sophomore year. We explain that we do not have answers to the questions, but they are meant to encourage them to think beyond the major. In the summer between their junior and senior year, students complete an internship abroad. When they come back, during their senior year, they have a second oral proficiency interview done by an outside tester, certified by the American Council on the Teaching of Foreign Languages. To get the certificate, students must show they have attained a much higher level of oral proficiency than when they came into the Center. Then they begin working on their senior integrative projects, which are essentially individual studies or honors theses within the major, put in the context of the three questions. We are currently considering whether to change the questions for the senior year, because we found that some of the students, in trying to find answers, merely repeated the answers they gave as sophomores. We are still working on this, but the goal is to constantly challenge the students to think outside the major, and to think of themselves as people who are not only preparing for a specific profession but to assume positions of responsibility in modern society.[1]

What we have been able to do is use the three traditions in harmony. For example, the whole idea of getting students to do research comes out of the Ph.D. research tradition. Students have an individual library mentor and one or two faculty advisors; the latter have Ph.D.s. Most students who have to do research in their majors must follow strict guidelines. In the process of going through the International Studies Certificate Program, they realize they are partaking of this research tradition. As far as the utilitarian tradition of having an education that will guarantee employment is concerned, we have been extremely successful. The students who have the certificate have done very well finding employment when they enter the job market, and those who pursue graduate work have done well. Having the oral proficiency, doing the internship abroad, and completing the senior integrative project matures them and gives them a certain presence. It also gives the interviewers something to talk about. Anyone who is interviewing a hundred thousand economics majors will focus on a student who was actually in Peru for a summer working on democracy and other critical issues.

The big question is, How well did we succeed in doing the liberal arts component? We will not know the answer for ten, 20, or 30 years. All we know at this point is that we preach a great deal, and the students get their certificates at the end of the year. The three Latin words *sapientia* (wisdom), *virtus* (virtue), and *eloquentia* (eloquence) appear on the certificate, as well as a passage from Cicero talking about what it means to have wisdom, and how one feels when the self is part of the whole and turns around to serve one's fellow citizens. We tell them: We have given you specific skills, but we expect you, later in life, to use those skills to make the world a better place.

From what the students tell us, the program has been immensely successful. My surprise, given the climate of the academic world and how critical and contentious we all can be, was that when I first talked about Cicero, wisdom, virtue, and eloquence, people did not get upset and say, "that's Eurocentric," or use some other argument. We actually discussed what language we should use on the certificate and considered representing all the languages of the world. Of course, we quickly realized we could not do it on one piece of paper. If we put it in Chinese, not everyone would understand it, and then someone would want to use an African language. Then we decided that since our liberal arts tradition comes from classical, especially Roman, antiquity, we should do the certificate in Latin. No one

---

1. Editor's note: As of fall 1996, there exist two sets of questions, one for the sophomore and junior years and one for the senior year.

complained. The surprising thing was that nobody was critical of the ideal of wisdom, virtue, and eloquence. Parents love it, and students like it.

What I have learned from this is that no matter how cynical and skeptical we are, certain traditions we inherit may make us who we are. People need ideals to live by, and for us that certainly is the motivating ideal. What kept us going was something inherently right in thinking about all the disciplines as complementary ways of understanding the whole. Thinking about the true meaning of our lives is the greater whole of which we are only a part, and maybe in the final analysis, happiness is related to rising above yourself and serving others. That certainly is what we try to teach in our program.

Part II

DYNAMIC MODELS:
PEDAGOGY AND PROGRAMS

Chapter 5

Beyond the Area Studies Wars

Neil Waters and David A. J. Macey

The new international studies major at Middlebury College is the result of a two-year gestation period. It almost died aborning for reasons that inevitably afflict any attempt to forge common ground among faculty with disparate theoretical orientations and regional loyalties.

The basic split, which brought our efforts in 1994-95 to a halt, is the classic one between globally oriented theorists and area-studies proponents. The former tend to look for commonalities at the human, rather than national or cultural level, and share, to varying degrees, these convictions:

- The world is getting smaller and more interdependent, and its inhabitants more alike.
- The growing similarity of economic conditions around the globe makes it possible to elicit a finite number of choices that people can make—whatever culture they come from.
- Transnational phenomena, including multinational corporations, international banking systems, trade agreements, and military security agreements are essential objects of study.

The area-studies proponents, the authors included, share varying degrees of these convictions:

- In many ways, the world is becoming increasingly fragmented rather than more homogenized—i.e., the collapse of the Soviet Union, the efforts of Quebec to secede from Canada, and the potential for neowarlordism in China.
- The homogenizing efforts of "rational-choice" theoreticians do a grave disservice to cultural specificity, involve circular thought, and ignore the inseparability of individuals from their cultural context. [1]

1. We discern a tautology in rational choice: All people employ rational rules to make choices; we search for the rules; we find rules; therefore all people are rational.

• Specific cultures should be the primary focus of study.

The participants in Middlebury's efforts to develop an international studies major were not extremists in these positions. The most "theoretical" globalist was not an unalloyed "rat-choicer," and the most confirmed area specialist did not deny the importance of transnational phenomena. Nevertheless, the differences were great enough to bring progress to a halt after a year.

What reignited our efforts in 1995-96 was the slowly dawning realization that victory for either camp would seriously undermine our efforts to produce students who could act effectively and positively in a variety of capacities in countries abroad and/or international organizations of all sorts. We area-studies types especially feared that students trained in theory to the exclusion of culture-specific experience and expertise would be the sort who would miss much that falls outside of theoretical models—the sort for whom such events as the fall of the Shah of Iran or Saddam Hussein's invasion of Kuwait would be as utterly surprising as these events in fact were to our own State Department and intelligence community. We also feared that the transformative aspects of immersion in another culture—the empathic capacity to perceive the world through eyes other than our own, and the concomitant ability to doubt our own centrality—would elude those who focused on transnational systems. Our more theoretically inclined colleagues feared that an area-studies victory would lead to involuted single-country specialists incapable of perceiving the common factors affecting, for example, the economic prospects of the newly industrialized counties (NICs) of East and Southeast Asia.

No grand intellectual breakthrough ensued, save perhaps for the idea that the people of Earth are undergoing both centrifugal and centripetal forces at the same time. There really are global or near-global economic phenomena that militate against some types of national particularism: Russians simply cannot enact and sustain a return to a highly subsidized state-economy, even if they would like to. At the same time, through "rediscovered" ethnic identity, religious revivalism, the intentional resurrection of "traditional" culture, the deliberate inculcation of nostalgia, or even the reincarnation of long-buried grievances, humans are proving very adept at finding new ways to reassert their identity on a scale small enough to be meaningful. Indeed, it would seem that the homogenizing effects of global interdependence act as a primary stimulus for the search for particular identity. Centripetal forces cause centrifugal reactions.

International studies programs have to address both the centripetal and centrifugal forces that affect and afflict us. This means that theorists and area specialists both have to eschew total victory and learn to cooperate. At Middlebury, we still eye each other warily from time to time, but we have been able to put together a careful blend of breadth and depth, language and overseas experience, expertise and theoretical sophistication.

Or so we would like to think. The balance will be put to the test during the next several years.

In practical terms, the compromise that was worked out and incorporated into the new major in International Studies (IS) combined the recognized, but more narrowly focused, strengths of the area-studies major with the broader, comparative, thematic, and cross-regional perspectives of traditional international studies programs. At the same time, we sought to overcome a second criticism of area studies as constituting a simple smorgasbord of courses by introducing a strong disciplinary focus in the liberal arts. We sought to recognize the shift in student interest from the traditional combination of foreign languages and literatures by combining language study with other disciplines, most notably history and the social sciences. Students will thus be able to combine virtually any discipline taught at Middlebury with both language and area study. And where regionally based courses in a given discipline are not offered at Middlebury, students will receive major credit for such courses taken abroad. Finally, in order to harness the oft-dissipated enthusiasm generated by study abroad, returning seniors will be brought together in a series of team-taught, interdisciplinary, comparative and/or cross-regional, and topically-focused senior seminars.

In addition to addressing curricular concerns, the structure of the IS major was also designed in part to allay fears of "proliferating majors," while simultaneously making possible the addition of new geographical areas. We reduced the total number of majors at Middlebury by folding three existing majors—Russian and East European Studies, East Asian Studies, and International Politics and Economics—into the new IS major, which pleased administrators immensely. Further, by designing and winning approval of a single curricular structure that is applicable to all regional foci, we were able to introduce two new programs or tracks virtually without opposition: Latin American Studies and European Studies. We anticipate that it will be a simple matter to add new regional foci in the future, if and when we add new languages during the regular academic year. At present, the most logical addition would be Middle Eastern studies, since we already teach Arabic during the summer.

Thus, the IS major will provide a carefully constructed blend of language, regional, disciplinary, and global courses that, together with Middlebury's traditional commitment to study abroad, seeks to impart to students a deep understanding of a specific geographical region (as defined primarily by language), as well as its place within an interdisciplinary and transnational context. Students who major in International Studies will share elements at the beginning and end of their college careers, with core courses and a senior capstone program. They will also have a wide variety of choices within the International Studies curriculum. For, in addition to specializing in one of the five programs that make up the major (East Asian Studies, European Studies, International Politics and Economics, Latin American

Studies, and Russian and East European Studies), they can choose to specialize in any one of the traditional liberal arts disciplines, while also studying abroad and achieving proficiency in one of the languages Middlebury teaches.

The minimum requirements for each of the six components of the major are as follows. For a schematic representation, see Table 5.1, "Middlebury College International Studies Major": [2]

- *The International Studies core:* Two introductory courses in international studies selected from among specially designated first-year Seminars, as well as introductory level courses in World History, International Politics, International Economics, Introduction to Anthropology, World Literatures, and World Regional Geography.
- *Language study:* Proficiency in Chinese, French, German, Italian, Japanese, Russian, or Spanish sufficient to do advanced work in that language.
- *Area specialization:* At least three courses (in three different departments) in one of the major's areas of geo-graphical focus, ideally taken before studying abroad.
- *Disciplinary specialization:* At least five courses in a single discipline. Within this disciplinary specialization, at least two courses must be in the geographical area of specialization, and if at all possible, such combined disciplinary/area courses should be taken on the Middlebury campus. Students will also be able to fulfill this requirement in language departments by focusing on literature and/or culture.
- *Study abroad:* For at least one semester (and preferably for a year) on a Middlebury-approved study-abroad program.
- *Senior program:* A regional and/or disciplinary senior seminar, as available; an advanced course—and preferably two—in the language of concentration; and an interdisciplinary and/or cross-regional, team-taught senior seminar. Students writing a two-semester senior thesis, however, will be exempt from the latter seminar.

---

2. The virtue of this template is its ability to clarify not only the common academic structure of each track within the major, but also the principal elements of the political compromises that had to be struck prior to its adoption.

Table 5.1
Middlebury College International Studies Major

Core*	Language and Culture*	Regional Specialization*	Disciplinary Specialization*	Study Abroad*	Senior Program*
Select 2 of the following (before going abroad)	Advanced study of a language taught at Middlebury[1]	3 courses in 3 different disciplines (before going abroad)	A minimum of 5 courses in one of the following disciplines	At least one semester and preferably a year	2 seminars and advanced study in a language
Intro to Anthropology	Chinese	East Asia	Economics	Middlebury programs	1 seminar in the discipline[2]
[International Economics]	French	Europe	Environmental Studies (joint major)	Other approved programs	1 topical multiregional seminar[3]
Introduction to Comparative Politics or International Politics	German	Latin America	Geography		Advanced study in a language[4]
Reading Literature	Italian	Russia and East Europe	History		Senior Thesis[5]
[World History]	Japanese	Other	History of Art and Architecture		
World Regional Geography	Russian		Literature/Culture: Chinese, French, German, Italian, Japanese, Latin American, Russian, Spanish		
Designated 1st-yr. seminars	Spanish		Music Philosophy Political Science Religion Sociology/Anthropology Film/Video Others[6]		

Table 5.1 (cont'd.)

Notes:

East Asian Studies—European Studies—International Politics & Economics—Latin American Studies—Russian & East European Studies

International Studies majors will concentrate in one of the above five programs, three of which currently exist as stand-alone majors. All five of the programs would have to conform to this international studies template. Specific structure and course content of those programs and of the various tracks in the program will be determined within the overall IS paradigm, by the relevant language and non-language division faculty. For example, currently East Asian Studies has a language-based "Japanese Track" and a "Chinese Track," while IP&E has a political science and economics track. We anticipate that the proposed European Studies and the Latin American Studies programs will develop tracks as they see fit.

* Individual courses may count for more than one category. Thus, if one were an IS/REES/History student, she would take HI247 and it would count both toward the regional and disciplinary specializations.

1. The number of semester courses will vary depending on the language. The language departments will establish the number of courses required to study abroad.

2. Each program within the International Studies major will designate the seminars that can be used to fulfill this requirement.

3. This seminar will be team-taught by two faculty who have different regional and/or disciplinary specializations. The goal of the seminar is to bring together students in international studies who have studied different regions and disciplines so they may share their expertise and gain a valuable comparative perspective on important issues that extend beyond a particular region.

4. Students must take at least one advanced course in the language, and are strongly encouraged to take two such courses.

5. Each program within the International Studies major will specify thesis requirements. Students who do a two-semester thesis are not required to complete the interdisciplinary seminar, though they are strongly encouraged to do so.

6. The Task Force does not wish to limit the disciplinary specialization choices to those disciplines that have regional offerings; thus, if a student wishes to do IS/German/Philosophy, she should be able to do so, and will be expected to take courses specific to the region (e.g., German philosophy) when she studies abroad.

Chapter 6

Reaching Moral and Cultural Maturity through International Studies

Julia A. Kushigian

In the education of our students, international studies programs must foster the development of and commitment to critical skills and ethical standards, for both personal enrichment and service in the international arena. Educators must create a dynamic structure capable of assessing what it means to study, coexist, think, research, and work internationally, without losing sight of ethical concerns. If we think of the liberal arts as a strategy for life, we will be prepared to meet this challenge, even as the ground keeps shifting. [1] The liberal arts tradition encourages us to see reality as a whole, with the different disciplines as complementary ways of viewing the whole. Moreover, it advocates rising above self-interest to work for the common good. The vigor of the liberal arts approach is that it affords a dialogue between tradition and modernity, as well as between ethical ideals and critical skills. At a time in our history when both modern civic engagement and traditional cultures offer vibrant solutions where revolutions and politics have failed, we encourage this liberating potential for dialogue. At stake is the idea that the tension between tradition and modernity will create a new space where a consensus between ethical and practical concerns can be forged.

---

1. In a publication entitled *In the International Interest: Contributions and Needs of America's International Liberal Arts Colleges*, the authors, David Engerman and Parker Marden, point to the strengths of a liberal arts education: "Many of the basic needs for international understanding are integral to a liberal arts education: the undermining of parochialism, the openness to change, the acquisition of effective communications skills, and the ability to see ideas in their full complexity. International awareness and commitment are logical extensions of what liberal arts colleges do in their special educational approach" (Engerman and Marden 1992, 19).

The need for ethical reflection as an integral part of an international studies program is evident from the recent case of cloning a sheep in Scotland, and the implications for an ethical debate already begun on human cloning. Our concern in an international studies program is to prepare students with the skills and motivation to enter such a debate and to speak and act responsibly, not only for themselves but for future generations. To encourage this debate on a practical level as well, we see the need for a central ethical dialogue regarding the practices of business firms, doctors, journalists, et cetera in "commerce" internationally. In fact, the complexities of life abroad can be as daunting to undergraduates engaged in overseas internships as they are for journalists, corporate CEOs, and physicians working in unfamiliar territory. Cultural differences and linguistic subtleties set up formidable obstacles to "doing the right thing." On a larger scale, policies of nations at odds because of differences in economic needs or principles of governance can also play havoc with good intentions. Such is the case when international art theft puts into question the concept of origin and ownership, or curable disease is rendered incurable due to incompatibility of medical documentation. This is also the case when fair business practices are uprooted and abandoned due to a lack of commonly held principles to guide the process.

The conflicts occasioned by the examples above are brought into the spotlight in times of natural disasters, ethnic battles, and extraordinary cases of inhumanity to men, women, and children. Sometimes, answers have been forthcoming, as in the Reverend Leon Sullivan's principles for doing business in South Africa under apartheid. These aided not only the residents of South Africa, but the businesses who responded to what they considered an invaluable moral guide. Of course, one set of principles might not translate well to another area, and sometimes workable ones are hard to find. Principles for doing business in China were attempted and abandoned by international trade groups in 1995. International studies programs might play an important role by beginning the process of exploring ethical principles transnationally for various fields, from biomedical research to the economic marketplace.

The need for ethical standards is painfully clear to the international business community, having experienced significant setbacks in the recent past. Due to a lack of consensus on values and standards, individuals and corporations have had to dedicate significant amounts of energy and funds to counteract allegations of wrongdoing and fight campaigns of misinformation waged against them. A list of recent cases includes: Raytheon, Inc. for alleged briberies in Brazil; CompuServe for access to material deemed immoral through the Internet in Germany; L'Oreal for allegedly cooperating with the Arab League's economic boycott of Israel; Freeport McMoRan for alleged payoffs in Indonesia; and Kathie Lee Gifford and Wal Mart Inc. for alleged infringements of labor standards in Honduras. For moral and economic reasons, what norms and standards should be enforced, which bodies should enforce them, and what should be applied in fields such as biomedical research, journalism, health services, and the arts?

Such principles can be so compelling as to inspire a proactive approach to associating with new communities and resolving differences. But a general consensus has not been reached on common values and standards in any field. Why? One stumbling block may be found, surprisingly, in the wide use of computer technology. The gains of the immediacy of contact coupled with the speed with which decisions can be made is offset by a greater potential for misjudgment when there is little or no time for reflection. Another obstacle is the push of information-driven societies to give global access to all materials, even those deemed insubstantial, illegal, immoral, or invalid by others. [2] According to Francis Fukuyama in his cogent study on trust and social virtues (1995, 10), "the ability to associate depends . . . on the degree to which communities share norms and values and are able to subordinate individual interests to those of larger groups. Out of such shared values comes trust."

The moral coherence we seek is grounded in a common set of values or global ethics. Trust and faithful relationships with each other, the law and civil society, are among the virtues we must share in order that human rights and standards of decency be guaranteed. International studies grounded in the liberal arts, with its inherently ethical orientation, prepares students with the critical skills and concern for the common good that encourages a resolution of problems incorporating a variety of perspectives.

FROM THEORY TO PRACTICE: INTERNATIONAL STUDIES AT CONNECTICUT COLLEGE

The Association of International Education Administrators in "A Research Agenda for the Internationalization of Higher Education in the United States" (1995) has put forth a number of comprehensive questions that provide a guide to outline our program at Connecticut College. These questions are: How are international programs funded and managed in our institutions of higher education? What faculty and other specialized resources are needed for effective internationalization? What programs and experiences have the most profound effect on the undergraduate attitudes and perceptions about cultural, economic, and political forces in the complex world they will inherit?

The Toor Cummings Center for International Studies and the Liberal Arts, also known as CISLA, offers an International Studies Certificate Program that embodies a liberal arts education for the twenty-first century. The program prepares students to face a complex, integrated, yet divided

---

2. Consequently, to offset the potential for error and misjudgment, it is helpful when trust guides the business or community alliance.

world, eschewing an ominous "dusk of nations" prophesied at the end of the last century by Max Nordau, for the joy of a creation, a celebration, or a regeneration. [3] Our program was designed to meet the need for individuals trained to use critical skills to solve problems, to think creatively, and enter the international arena with a good academic base of knowledge, foreign work experience, and language fluency. Unlike preprofessional or graduate programs dedicated to research, public policy, or business skills, our program internationalizes the student's major with a firm base in the liberal arts. Our students study an area of the world in an interdisciplinary fashion, develop foreign language proficiency and an understanding of another culture, work in that culture and language, and then return to think and write about their experiences in a senior integrative project. The program is intercultural and interdisciplinary in nature.

To enter the program, Connecticut College students begin a rigorous and competitive application process in their sophomore year. Students must provide evidence of their commitment to internationalizing their major and demonstrate their research and internship goals, proficiency in a foreign language, and an understanding of some of the concerns of the international community. Faculty trained by the American Council on the Teaching of Foreign Languages, Inc. (ACTFL) interview students for proficiency at entry level in one of the seven foreign languages taught at the college (Chinese, French, German, Italian, Japanese, Russian, Spanish) or any other language, provided they will be able to improve their language skills in the absence of courses on campus.

Once admitted to the program, our students sign the CISLA pledge and challenge. They pledge to reach a higher, required level of oral proficiency in the foreign language; to take seminars on the origins and dynamics of modern global society; to explore one region of the world and its culture in four core courses; to complete one workshop a year in critical skills such as public speaking, negotiation, interviewing, or computers; to complete a funded summer internship in the field, country, and culture of his or her choice; and finally, to complete a senior research project that integrates the internship, the major, and the foreign language. [4] With the guidance of the Center director, associate directors, and faculty advisors, CISLA scholars meet the challenge, see something of the world, gain some understanding of foreign cultures, discover their strengths and limitations, learn self-reliance, and think about the meaning and purpose of life so they may live well and wisely in a rapidly changing and interdependent world. Our goal, to paraphrase Giambattista Vico, is to provide a truly human

---

3. See Sylvia Molloy's article, "Too Wilde for Comfort: Desire and Ideology in fin de siècle Spanish America," *Social Text*, 1992, 10: 2-3 (31-32), 187-201.

4. Our internships are funded by The Toor Cummings Center. The student does not generally receive a salary. Jobs are full-time positions that last from eight to 12 weeks depending upon the employer.

education, one that focuses on particular issues, while never losing sight of the general background or context that gives these issues meaning or importance—that is to say, one that sets the stage for a dialogue across time, contextualizing global concerns and theories. [5]

STUDENT CASE HISTORIES

The stories of CISLA scholars Maria Recchia and Matthew Tanner add life to our description of goals. Maria was a Dean's list, zoology major, who studied Italian as her second language, volunteered as a tutor at New London High School, and worked for a clean environment. Not a native speaker of Italian, she was ranked at the intermediate-high level during her entrance interview, and at the advanced level during the exit interview. Maria was given an internship at the Stazione Zoologica Anton Dohrn in Naples, Italy, which was the first research station of its kind when established in 1872. She spent her summer in this historic landmark, raising copepod larvae from eggs to adults and examining their various stages of development. The larvae were obtained from zooplankton samples collected by fishermen associated with the Stazione.

In her three months at the Stazione, Maria worked on her own project, observed work underway in the other laboratories, and went on a plankton collecting excursion with the scientists and fishermen. The latter part was perhaps the most challenging for Maria, both linguistically and culturally. She was determined to accompany the fishermen as they prepared their boats late at night and early into the morning for the excursion. Since, as we all know, "nice" girls do not go down to the docks at night and women certainly do not do this kind of manual labor, Maria had to be very persuasive in convincing the fishermen to allow her to become a part of their work. In fact, when conducting interviews with the people of the village of Piano di Sorrento, a traditional southern Italian fishing community, Maria was told that, "fishermen fish and women and others grow plants."

In the laboratory, the persuasion required to work on her own project was of a different nature. The scientists were unaccustomed to working with undergraduates who were as skilled and mature as Maria. The broad implications of her case study began to develop as she combated cultural, social, gender, and research biases. Maria's supervisor and collaborator on her project gave her kudos for her competence, patience, and intelligence, qualities needed to ensure success in any field under such difficult conditions. Upon reviewing our internship requirement, the supervisor applauded a program that "gives such a broad background in science and humanities," and then went on to ask, "Can I apply?"

5. Taken from Giambattista Vico's inaugural oration, 1704, in which he tried to convince parents and students of the benefits of humanistic education in the liberal arts.

Maria's senior integrative project, "A Study of the Effects of Industrialization on the Marine Ecosystem of the Italian Mediterranean," was completed her senior year. Her project, incorporating her research on zooplankton samples and interviews with and a sociological study of the fishing community, borders on the lyrical in an excursion through cultural, gender, social, and sociological differences. Maria is presently completing a Masters in Natural Resources and Environmental Studies at Dalhousie University in Halifax, Canada. Prior to returning for graduate studies, she did consulting on environmental education and curriculum development for various clients in New England.

Matthew Tanner was an international relations major and economics minor. Russian is his second language. Even without the benefit of study abroad, Matt had ranked at the intermediate-mid level during his entrance interview. Feeling unchallenged during his first internship in Moscow, when the city was in a period of flux and democratization, Matt approached the Moscow Chamber of Commerce for a list of American companies doing business there. He contacted the firm of Ernst & Young, which was in the process of privatizing a mine in Mongolia. Matt interviewed, and was immediately asked to travel to Mongolia to translate for a group of American accountants, who spoke no Russian, and a guide whose business card simply read "expert." The group drove through the desert, passing caravans of camels and small villages. Matt tells how at one point their car broke down and horsemen stopped to fashion a fan belt out of reins.

Matt spent over two months at the mines, working as an official translator. Upon completion of the job, he returned with the team to Moscow to write up a report on their work. Ernst & Young was so impressed with Matthew Tanner that upon graduation they offered him a full-time position. Although based in New York, Matt returns to Russia on business several times a year.

QUESTIONS TO STIMULATE SYNTHESIS

What does our program provide that has helped Matthew Tanner, Maria Recchia, and others accomplish their goals and integrate their experiences into a constructive outlook on a world in flux? CISLA scholars complete two seminars, one during the sophomore year, entitled "Perspectives on Modern Global Society," and a senior seminar after the internship. In the seminars, students explore a set of three questions that form the overarching theoretical framework of their intellectual exercises during their tenure as CISLA scholars. [6] No one has expressed the purpose of these questions better than our founding director, Robert Proctor, when he said: "These questions open students to something larger than themselves. They invite

---

6. In the fall of 1996, a set of questions was added to the senior experience to respond to the debate between internationalization and area studies.

students to ponder the modern world as a whole, in part by stepping outside of it and looking at it from the perspective of the past. They challenge students to expand their horizons by taking in the viewpoints of other people and other cultures, including those of past ages. And they encourage students to think about the civic responsibilities of their education" (Proctor 1995, 15).

The questions explored by sophomores and juniors are: What are the origins and dynamics of contemporary society? What are the differences between a traditional and a modern society? What are the material and spiritual challenges of modernity? Questions examined by the seniors are: Is there a modern global society/global village? Defend your answer. What can we gain from a dialogue with the past? What are the ethical challenges to modernity? The question on the origins and dynamics of contemporary society relates to the question on modern global society. Both invite students to debate whether we have a modern global society, and if so, how it came into being. In his book *Jihad vs. McWorld,* Benjamin Barber refers to modern society as a global theme park tied together by communications, information, entertainment, and the commerce that forges global markets. Evidence of Barber's vision is everywhere, from the McDonald's in Moscow or the Kentucky Fried Chicken at the Great Wall of China, rap music in Brazil, EuroDisney in France, and the Zapatistas with a web page. Students are asked to consider that if the surface of our lives has been globalized, what are some of the underlying causes.

The question on a dialogue with the past speaks to the differences between traditional and modern societies. What do people have to gain from a dialogue with the history and traditions of their nation or tribe, or ethnic or religious group? Mexican novelist and advocate of civil society, Carlos Fuentes, concludes the following: "The ruin of Modernity does not mean the end of time but the challenge to create a new text, rising from the ruins, and to do it not in the suicidal rejection of tradition but precisely in the tension between tradition and creation" (Fuentes 1993). Our dialogue with the past must explore that tension between tradition and creation to take advantage of the potential for human reason.

The final question of both groups challenges students to develop a moral consciousness in addition to a historical one: What are the material, spiritual, and ethical challenges of modernity? Hannah Arendt has used the term *moral maturity* to explain the meaning of goodwill, which she calls a willingness to welcome diversity as an enrichment and to approach others in openness, seeking a common ground. I use the term *cultural maturity* for the ability to leave what is secure and familiar and open oneself to the Other. This entails understanding cultural and linguistic differences, and then returning home, enriched by the relationship to the Other and a deeper understanding of the self. Language teachers love to highlight the importance of language by telling the story about the sign in an elevator in Paris that declared, "Please feel free to leave your values in the hotel's safe."

At Connecticut College we exhort our students to carry their values with them instead of leaving them in a dark, enclosed space, so as to demonstrate the moral and cultural maturity we know they are capable of displaying.

CAMPUS-WIDE COMMITMENT

What support does a program like ours need to succeed? First and foremost it needs support from the administration. As a center, it is funded entirely outside the college's budget, but the initiative must receive support from the central administration to the office of development. Fund raising is a primary concern, to get support from private and public sources and foundations to pay for start-up funds, program development, operating expenses, and internships. Being outside the college's budget gives the Center the flexibility it needs to respond quickly and aggressively to the changes in the international community.

Pedagogically, we require the commitment of the foreign language faculty to support the needs of students in the foreign language, but outside the traditional language and literature majors. We also ask them to learn the techniques of rating oral proficiency as espoused by ACTFL. The goal is to be able to interview candidates for entry into our program, but also to instruct a new generation of language learners in oral and written proficiency.

For our program to have a campus-wide impact, every department, every discipline must be able to participate. If we are asking students to internationalize their majors, we must first have the faculty who are willing and able to support the students who choose to take up the challenge. To date, we have never had to turn away a student because a department could not or would not support the student's interest. The administration is committed to internationalizing the faculty as well as the curriculum. The college's policies in hiring, tenure, and promotion stimulate and reward cross-disciplinary teaching, pedagogical and technological experimentation, and faculty development in foreign languages and cultures. This accounts for the success with faculty and students of our Foreign Languages Across the Curriculum (FLAC) Program, which was funded by a grant from the U.S. Department of Education.

Another part of our strategy is to hire faculty proficient in languages not taught at the college. These faculty members serve as cultural resources and linguistic support in languages that may be the focus of the next millennium.

Finally, the college has sought diversity in the student body, as well as the faculty. We recognize the imperative for international studies programs to address the underrepresented groups who typically are not foreign language majors or minors. According to a survey by the Institute of International Education, 83.8 percent of students who studied abroad last year were white, 8 percent Hispanic, 5 percent Asian, 2.8 percent African

American, .3 percent native American, and 3.1 percent multiracial. Female students have traditionally outnumbered males by a margin of about two to one. [7] In the fall of 1995, our Center admitted a class of CISLA scholars comprised of 54 percent women and 46 percent men. Currently, 14 percent are students of color. These students have brought four new majors to the Center—American studies, philosophy, biochemistry, and architectural studies—and three new languages—Danish, Hebrew, and Polish—added to those mastered off-campus by our students. [8]

From its inception, the support for our program has come from the top. In an article in a 1994 issue of *Educational Record*, the president of the college, Dr. Claire Gaudiani, wrote about the considerable changes she believes higher education must make in order to succeed in the next century: "Faculty members amenable to such reform will need administrators who make the reward system reflect the high value society and the academic institution place on the changes. Faculty also will need the opportunities, encouragement, time, and funds necessary to learn new skills, technologies, and fields, and to take risks and develop a new consensus about the purposes of education and the role of educated American citizens in the twenty-first century" (Gaudiani 1994).

In the twenty-first century, our students will be called upon to translate complex material into common, everyday metaphors, in English as well as other languages, for the benefit of the general public. Connecticut College's mandate is to link critical skills to ethical concerns in an international, interdisciplinary, and intercultural context. In this setting, we believe we have devised a structure for shaping knowledgeable, competent, imaginative citizens, and public intellectuals who can live and work in ways that will promote international justice, security, and quality of life. [9]

REFERENCES

"A Research Agenda for the Internationalization of Higher Education in the United States." Recommendations and Report of the Association of International Education Administrators, August 1995.

Barber, Benjamin R. 1995. *Jihad vs. McWorld: How the Planet is Both Falling Apart and Coming Together and What this Means for Democracy.* New York: Times Books.

---

7. The statistics are taken from a survey by the Institute of International Education and a publication entitled *Education for Global Competence: Report of the Advisory Council for International Educational Exchange.* New York: Council on International Educational Exchange, August 1988.

8. Other underrepresented languages studied by CISLA scholars in the past are Arabic, Czech, Dutch, Portuguese, Wolof, and Swahili.

9. See also the product of another project of The Toor Cummings Center reflecting international interests, democracy, and ethical concerns, *Democracy is a Discussion: Civic Engagement in Emerging Democracies.*

Engerman, David C. and Parker G. Marden. 1992. *In the International Interest: Contributions and Needs of America's Liberal Arts Colleges.* Beloit, Wisconsin: International Liberal Arts Colleges.

Fuentes, Carlos. 1993. "Impossible." Inaugural Address at the "Present and Future of Mexican Literature" Symposium. Guadalajara, Mexico.

Fukuyama, Francis. 1995. *Trust: The Social Virtues and the Creation of Prosperity.* New York: The Free Press.

Gaudiani, Claire L. 1994. "For a New World, A New Curriculum." *Educational Record* (winter): 23.

Proctor, Robert E. 1995. "Grounding International Studies in the Liberal Arts Tradition," *ADFL Bulletin* 27 (fall): 15.

Chapter 7

The All-University Curriculum: A Team-Teaching, Interdisciplinary, and Inter-College Approach

Joan O'Mara, Jane Horvath, Marcia Seabury,
Harald Sandstrom, and Susan Coleman

Internationalizing the curriculum and campus has been a strategic goal for the University of Hartford since the mid-1980s. It is a private, comprehensive university located in West Hartford, Connecticut, serving approximately 4,000 undergraduates and 2,000 graduate students. In pursuit of internationalization, the university has:

- enrolled approximately 600 international students, representing 70 different countries each year;
- developed study abroad relationships that allow students to live, travel, and study in over 20 countries;
- offered courses in seven languages and cultures;
- supported faculty professional development through travel, seminars, hosting international faculty, and grants for research and curricular projects;
- established a permanently funded and staffed International Center in 1992 to serve as the focal point for international activities on campus.

In addition, between 1992 and 1994, an interdisciplinary team of faculty worked to develop an International Studies Degree within the College of Arts & Sciences. This program is now up and running. A key component of the degree, and the core curriculum for the university as a whole, is the All-University Curriculum (AUC), which was introduced in 1987.

The AUC predates the International Studies Degree by a number of years. As such, it represents an example of how the university has adapted an existing component of the curriculum to meet its goal to internationalize. Rather than develop an entirely new group of courses, the university "internationalized" courses that were an accepted part of the curriculum and began the process of "internationalizing" the faculty teaching those courses.

CAPITALIZING ON THE TEAM APPROACH

The AUC, celebrating its tenth anniversary in 1997, was designed to include interdisciplinary and team-taught courses that would stimulate critical thinking, oral and written communication, civic responsibility, and values identification through active learning. Since its inception, the AUC has grown to encompass approximately 30 courses falling into five categories:

- Living in a Cultural Context: Western Heritage
- Living in a Cultural Context: Other Cultures
- Living Responsively to the Arts
- Living in a Social Context
- Living in a Scientific and Technological World

All students are required to take a minimum of four AUC courses from four different categories prior to graduation. Typically, these courses are taken during the freshman and sophomore years, becoming an important part of the student's core curriculum.

The AUC has become a major vehicle for internationalizing the curriculum and exposing all students to other people's cultures and countries. Some AUC courses, such as "The Caribbean Mosaic" and "Discovering Britain," are explicitly international. Others, such as "Hunger: Problems of Scarcity and Choice" and "Cultures and Transnational Corporations," address international and global issues within a comparative framework.

Since the AUC is interdisciplinary, students develop the habit of looking at issues from multiple perspectives, a step in working toward cross-cultural understanding. Moreover, most AUC courses specifically raise cross-cultural issues. For example, in "Sex, Society, and Selfhood," the issue of growing up male and female in different countries is addressed. In "Ethnic Roots and Urban Arts," the cultures of American cities are explored. Because of the diverse offerings within the AUC, students have the choice of viewing international and multicultural issues from a variety of vantage points. There is no single mandated international course that everyone must take in order to be properly imbued with cultural understanding.

Because AUC courses are team-taught by faculty from different disciplines, the courses stimulate interdisciplinary conversations across colleges. Full-time faculty—not a separate cadre of faculty for interdisciplinary general education—from the nine colleges in the university participate. Senior and junior faculty, grounded in their various disciplines, bring the richness of their experience and knowledge to this collaboration and to students who are non-majors. Faculty teams meet to plan and develop courses, pooling the perspectives of their respective disciplines and viewing material in new ways through the interconnections and synergy of the team. Many faculty teams meet regularly throughout the semester. Arguments and disagreements that might arise in class only serve to illustrate that different and acceptable views exist on many issues.

The AUC allows for course continuity combined with opportunities for change, growth, and professional development. The team model facilitates effective orientation and training for new faculty. This feature is particularly important for courses incorporating international content, since faculty may be hesitant to take the plunge into teaching less familiar international and comparative material. By working in teams, they have other experts on hand to try out new ideas. The team model has helped to incorporate new ideas, materials, and activities into the curriculum. Summer workshops for AUC faculty encourage teams to experiment together, share ideas and continue to stretch. As new faculty members join existing teams, their new perspectives on the course and its content have a kaleidoscopic effect.

THREE COURSES ILLUSTRATE AUC IN ACTION

"Hunger: Problems of Scarcity and Choice" was added to the university curriculum in 1987 as one of the first courses in the AUC. Offered each semester during the academic year, enrollment runs from 75 to 125 students per semester. This course is a mainstay of the "Other Cultures" category, and is one of the most popular in the program. Like most courses in the AUC, this one is interdisciplinary and team-taught. The team typically consists of an anthropologist, a biologist, an economist, and a philosopher. Students register for a section taught by an individual instructor. Sections are capped at 25 students, with a minimum of three sections each semester. The class meets for 75-minute sessions twice weekly, once in a large group of all sections combined and once in small groups led by the individual instructors.

While one instructor has primary responsibility for a particular large group session, the other members of the team assist in planning. The multidisciplinary nature of the discussions is brought out by the discipline-based team members. There is often intense interaction among instructors during large group sessions, and students learn that this is part of the process of coming to terms with the material. Faculty debate points, ask questions, and may disagree among themselves on a variety of issues. In turn, students are encouraged to be active participants and discouraged from sitting back. Team members encourage, anger, and cajole students into speaking out and debating issues.

The small group sessions provide the opportunity for students who are comfortable in more intimate settings to participate. These sessions tend to generate more in-depth discussion about the readings and issues raised in the larger groups. Quizzes, exams, and presentations of group and individual projects typically take place during the small group meetings.

The hunger course is designed to give students an understanding of the problem of hunger—its causes and possible remedies. Food production problems are distinguished from food distribution problems, and famine is differentiated from chronic persistent hunger, which is related to disease, health care, and drug-resistant microbes. The roles of technology, pollution, and population growth are also explored. Through the course, students begin to understand the concept of global interdependence. The course is structured to make students aware that hunger, poverty, disease, and pollution in distant parts of the world have and will continue to have an impact on them.

The course begins in the developing world, where most of the hungry live. It tries to establish the students' connection to the problems of hunger, both in terms of causes and effects. Links are established between poverty in the developing world, the developed world, the United States, Connecticut, and finally, Hartford. Ending with Hartford reinforces the notion that hunger is not something disconnected and foreign from the students' experience.

This course exposes students to many disciplines and cultures. Perhaps the most rewarding aspect of the course is that students gain an appreciation for what it means to be citizens of the world and how much our actions affect others. As a result of this course, many students have gone on to do volunteer work in the community and to study abroad.

Like the hunger course, "Cultures and Transnational Corporations," which was first offered in 1988, falls within the "Other Cultures" category and is multidisciplinary, team-taught, and offered each semester. Typically, 50 to 75 students are enrolled in two to three sections. Faculty in the disciplines of English (comparative literature) and International Economics and Political Science teach (and are compensated for teaching) their own sections, but also integrate their individual sections into the large group sessions to benefit from the cross-fertilization of ideas.

The course uses international business as a vehicle for studying other cultures. We have to emphasize this approach, because every semester, business students come into the course expecting to learn the nuts and bolts of multinational business. We try not to scare them away, because, of course, business people need to understand the cultures in which they operate.

The original objective of the course was to expose students to "the interactions between multinational corporations and the foreign environments in which they operate, with special emphasis on the cultural dimension and its political effects." The faculty became sensitive to the xenophobic ring of terms, such as "foreign" or "other," used in conjunction with "cultures." We recognized that the original intent to expose students to a culture other than their own assumed most students to be Euro-Americans, and that the international economy was becoming globalized. Our solution was to change the name of the course from "Foreign Cultures and Multinational Corporations" to "Cultures and Transnational Corporations," and move away from a focus on European topics, such as the European Community, and toward inclusion of the Pacific Rim (i.e., "The Four Little Dragons" of South Korea, Taiwan, Singapore, and Hong Kong), South America, and the Caribbean.

Throughout the course, efforts are made to sensitize students to cultural diversity. We try to impress upon students that time is not perceived or acted upon the same way everywhere, and that people have different values toward work and leisure. Personal and family relations may have priority over closing a business deal. Nationalist sensitivities, understandable in the face of colonial exploitation and continuing domination by highly advanced, Western capitalist states, must be acknowledged.

Perhaps the greatest challenge in offering this course is reflected in the personal growth of the faculty. The end of the Cold War, the subsequent emergence of market and mixed economies in the former socialist states, and the equally dramatic change in South Africa have provided new challenges and opportunities to the faculty. Already extending themselves beyond their disciplinary training in teaching the AUC courses, faculty have had to work even harder to develop new course material incorporating the massive global changes that are generally not covered in the texts. But the greatest reward has been in the camaraderie and mutual support among team members, and in the response of students whose appreciation for "other" ways of doing things has been enhanced. Faculty are convinced that students who develop a greater sensitivity to international differences will also be better prepared to work in the increasingly diverse domestic workplace.

"The Caribbean Mosaic" is the most recently developed of the AUC courses covered here. Due to its diversity, the Caribbean is an excellent region to study. The course examines both commonalities and differences among the various countries in the region in geography, language, religion, economic development, history, politics, race and class, literature, art, and music. The contributions of different groups including Amerindians, Western Europeans, Africans, Asians, Indians, and Middle Easterners are explored, along with broad themes such as monoculture, slavery, colonialism, exploitation, and migration.

One of the books students read and discuss for the course is *The Tragedy of King Christophe*, a play by the Martinican playwright Aime Cesaire. It addresses race and class, slavery, language, voodoo, revolution, European intervention, and independence and can be analyzed from an historical perspective. However, the play is also a literary work and an excellent vehicle for discussing tragedy, satire, character development, and motivation.

After reading and discussion, the class is divided into smaller groups to present a staged reading of a portion of the play. As parts are chosen, students are urged to put themselves in the places of the characters they are portraying. Many of the groups bring in props and costumes to help bring their characters to life. According to the students, this dramatic reading gives them a better understanding of the play, of Haiti and the Caribbean. It also provides grounding for a discussion of current problems in Haiti.

Student outcomes, based on journal entries and exam essays from the spring semester of 1996, show an increased interest in various aspects of Caribbean culture and a greater understanding of the region. One student wrote:

The region receives very little, if any, publicity in the American mainstream [media] as anything other than a tourist attraction. But after a class like this one, my summer visit will mean more to me than simply a pilgrimage to the Mecca of vacation land. For this, I am appreciative for having taken this class. . . . This class would allow me, and will this summer, to look upon the region with more of an appreciation of the area. . . . Upon my trip to Jamaica, I will be able to understand more fully the history and strife that made the island what it is today.

Student feedback attests to a greater appreciation for the region's history, art, music, literature, and culture, and to a greater understanding of the complexities and richness behind the one-dimensional travel posters, which may have been their only association with the Caribbean prior to this course.

When the University of Hartford faced the task of internationalizing courses across the curriculum, it chose to internationalize existing courses that lent themselves to international perspectives, rather than creating new courses. This strategy has proven advantageous in both curriculum development and faculty professional development. By internationalizing existing AUC courses, faculty do not have to clear the hurdles of new course approval, nor do they have to introduce new courses which may draw resources and enrollments away from existing ones.

The All-University Curriculum is well-known and widely accepted by students, faculty, and the administration. Faculty interaction in course preparation and in the classroom enriches the content and provides a living example of the complexities that are part of global awareness, appreciation, and understanding.

SUGGESTED READINGS

Adams, Maurianne, ed. "Promoting Diversity in College Classrooms: Innovative Responses for the Curriculum, Faculty, and Institutions." *New Directions for Teaching and Learning* 52. San Francisco: Jossey-Bass, 1992.

American Council of Education. *Educating Americans for a World in Flux: Ten Ground Rules for Internationalizing Higher Education.* Washington, D.C., 1995.

Audas, Millie C. "Comparing Policy Statements and Practices in the International Dimension of Selected Institutions of Higher Education, Part 1." *International Education Forum* (fall 1990): 59-73.

Council on International Educational Exchange. *Educating for Global Competence: The Report of the Advisory Council for International Educational Exchange.* New York, 1988.

Davis, James R. *Interdisciplinary Courses and Team Teaching: New Arrangements for Learning.* Phoenix: ACE/Oryx, 1995.

El-Khawas, Elaine. "Toward a Global University: Status and Outlook in the United States." *Higher Education Management* 6, no. 1 (March 1994): 90-98.

————. *Campus Trends 1995: New Directions for Academic Programs.* Washington, D.C.: American Council on Higher Education, 1995.

Hoemeke, Thomas H. "Education for International Competence and Competitiveness: The Texan Response." *International Education Forum* (fall 1990): 74-85.

Lambert, Richard D. "International Studies and Education: The Current State of Affairs." *International Education Forum* (spring 1990): 1-8.

Lombardi, John V. "America International: Colleges, Universities, and Global Education." *International Education Forum* (spring 1991): 1-8.

Pickert, Sarah M. *Preparing for a Global Community: Achieving an International Perspective in Higher Education.* ASHE-ERIC Higher Education Report No. 2. Washington, D.C.: George Washington University, 1992.

Schechter, Michael G. "Internationalizing the Undergraduate Curriculum." *International Education Forum* (spring 1990): 14-20.

Wright, Sheila. "Promoting Intellectual Development During the Freshman Year." *Journal of the Freshman Year Experience* 4, no. 2 (1992): 23-39.

Chapter 8

Weaving International Perspectives into the Fabric of a College Community

M. Kathleen Mahnke, Kathleen Rupright, and Bonnie Tangalos

The title of this chapter uses imagery, which represents a strategic choice for an institution of higher learning today. Many of us at Saint Michael's College are working to create a multicultural tapestry of the college community. We have always believed that students from all countries of the world must be exposed to languages and cultures outside their own as an integral part of their education. However imperfectly we are able to define the term globalization, it is evident that we are hurtling toward a new order, a new way in which the world—at least in many of its important aspects—is being organized. To function, let alone be effective, our educated can only deem themselves as such if they have been so exposed, trained, and nurtured.

Saint Michael's, known as the International University of Vermont, is a small, Catholic, liberal arts college located in Colchester, with 1,700 undergraduate students, 700 graduate students, and, at any given time during the year, at least 100 international students studying English. During the summer, the campus is host to 700 international students in English language and culture programs, as well as to a Master of Arts in Teaching English as a Second Language Program. The School of International Studies (SIS), in which these programs are housed, has a long-shared history with the rest of the college.

In 1954, an intensive English program, one of the first in the United States, was begun at Saint Michael's. The interest in language teaching is perhaps attributable to the Edmundite Fathers, founders of the college. The Edmundites were French speakers who came to Vermont via Quebec and had to learn English themselves, making the campus culture hospitable to language teaching and learning from the outset. The program grew rapidly and has served thousands of students from all parts of the globe.

In 1958, the Master of Arts in Teaching English as a Second Language Program was initiated, also one of the first in the United States. The English language programs of the School of International Studies have recently celebrated 42 years of continuous operation with 15,000 alumni from 65 different countries.

While the SIS, then known as the Center for International Programs, was building this impressive record, the rest of the college community hardly knew it existed. It was not located on the main campus, and the international students who flocked to Saint Michael's were rarely involved in college-wide activities. The faculty of the SIS was similarly isolated. Domestic undergraduate students were hardly aware of the presence of international students, let alone the benefits of the multicultural diversity in their midst. All of that began to change when Dr. Paul Reiss became president of the institution in 1985. His appointment coincided with a national trend toward the globalization/internationalization of American college campuses. President Reiss saw the great potential of the SIS to become an important element in the growth of the college. In his strategic plan, he made a strong case for integrating it into the academic structure and community of the college. The SIS moved to the main campus in 1987. A blueprint for the globalization of the campus was prepared in 1995, and a set of action plans was formulated.

However, one cannot legislate change from the top. Strategic plans are helpful, but to be successful, an initiative of this sort must be a bottom-up effort—and at Saint Michael's, it was. A variety of language-across-the-curriculum initiatives, designed to interweave internationalization into the curriculum, began in 1988, when the college received a grant from the Consortium for the Advancement of Private Higher Education. The grant helped underwrite faculty development geared toward fostering an intercultural dimension in academic programs.

The project, which involved intensive Japanese language study and a four-week trip to Japan for seven faculty members, allowed the college to add some depth in Japanese culture to various courses in the humanities. While the effort was helpful in initiating efforts toward internationalization, it did little to involve our own international school, which the college was just beginning to realize represented a unique resource.

At this juncture, Saint Michael's learned about a grant offered by the American Council on Education and the National Endowment for the Humanities to work with a mentor institution to establish languages-across-the-curriculum projects. The college received one of these grants, and was selected to participate in a program called Spreading the Word. Saint Michael's was paired with a mentor team at Saint Olaf College in Northfield, Minnesota. In 1992, the dean of Saint Michael's and two faculty attended a workshop for mentor and mentored institutions, followed by a visit to Saint Olaf to observe programs and meet with mentors. The Saint Olaf team subsequently came to Saint Michael's to consult.

THREE WORKING MODELS

The outcome of this interaction has been the design of a number of new course models. In our attempt to reach the largest number of international and domestic students, whose experiences with languages vary considerably, faculty in the SIS and the Department of Modern Languages developed three distinct models. While they differ in form and content, all offer at least one applied-language component (an optional, one-hour-a-week course conducted in the target language), or one cross-cultural component (an optional, one-hour-a-week course designed to increase student awareness of cultural differences in specific contexts).

Model I includes both domestic and international students, and is designed to demonstrate the value of building on language skills to increase awareness of other cultures to domestic undergraduate students, who are required to have a minimum of two years of high school foreign language study. These students do not need to be currently studying a language. This model is also designed to give international students a way to practice their English within a cognitively demanding academic setting.

Model I is led by discipline faculty, faculty from the SIS, and graduate student language-resource specialists. The discipline professor teaches the content course. The professor from the SIS and the language-resource specialist, a graduate student in the Master of Arts in Teaching English as a Second Language Program, attend the regular sessions of the course and lead a cross-cultural component. Extra reading and discussions in a cross-cultural component in Model I courses are conducted primarily in English for the benefit of international students. Basic vocabulary and structure from all of the languages represented in the class are explored as well. One extra English credit is offered to international students for their work in the component class; domestic students earn one extra credit in the discipline.

To benefit both international and domestic students, the course is designed to include linguistic and cultural information relevant to the discipline area. Much of this information is provided by the international students themselves. These students come from a variety of language backgrounds, including Spanish, French, Japanese, Russian, Thai, Chinese, Eastern European, and German. The interchange between American and international students provides a foundation for promoting greater interest in the study of other languages and cultures. International students improve their academic language proficiency in English, experience closer academic integration, and act as information givers, not just receivers. The course also serves to enhance these students' self-esteem, which tends to suffer in an unfamiliar environment, isolated from others by invisible boundaries. Implementation of this model was funded by the Department of Education, Center for International Education in 1994. During the two years of the grant, Principles of Microeconomics and Modern Latin America were offered as Model I courses.

Model II classes provide students who are studying French, German, Italian, Japanese, Russian, or Spanish an opportunity to use these languages in a content area. It has two versions derived from our own experiments in incorporating languages into content areas and from the successful Saint Olaf College applied-foreign-language component model. The courses are designed to serve students who have already attained a prescribed level of language proficiency.

There are two versions of Model II. The first version involves one professor teaching both the discipline course and the applied-language component. For the past decade, professors from the Department of Modern Languages have taught some culture courses in English as a part of the college humanities offerings. Language students often enroll in these courses, desiring to learn more about the people and places where a language is spoken. We found students eager to enroll in an applied-language component attached to one of these courses, entitled "Latin American Culture and Civilization." From among the 26 students enrolled in the course, we recruited ten for a Spanish applied-language component. These students met for one hour a week to discuss assigned Spanish readings that complemented the English texts assigned for the regular course. Another experiment with applied language took place in the spring semester of 1993 in "Latino Cultures in the United States." Fifteen students enrolled in this component course. These courses have been so successful that we have continued with the model, adding "Italian Culture," "Russian Culture," and "Quebec Cinema" to the list of offerings.

The second version of Model II is taught by two professors, one teaching the discipline course, the other, the applied-language component. One of the professors is in a discipline and one is from the Department of Modern Languages. Working in collaboration, the discipline professor and the language professor select foreign language texts that complement the English texts. These readings offer different perspectives on course topics. The students meet with the language professor for one hour a week to discuss assigned readings, receiving one credit in the language in addition to the regular number of credits for the discipline course. Graduate student language-resource specialists who have experience in the language and in content-based language instruction may work with the professors.

Model III is a discipline course with multiple applied-language components. The format of this course is a combination of Models I and II. From Model I comes the concept of commingling domestic and international students. From Model II comes the concept of practice in target languages. Model III will include applied-language components in French, German, Italian, Japanese, Russian, and Spanish. With a 1996 grant from the Department of Education, we offered a Model III course, "Literature of the Americas," using literature and language to study North, South, and Central America. We are planning to offer a Model III course in human geography, which considers social, economic, political, and linguistic influences on the nature of places and the development of human identity within a culture.

In the geography course, the professor will teach the content material, with French, German, Japanese, Russian, and Spanish professors attending these classes. The language professors, with language-resource specialists, will then lead weekly applied-language components. Primary texts, such as newspapers and periodicals, as well as personal narratives, and documentary and feature films like *El Norte* and *Journey of Hope*, will be used in these weekly meetings. These texts will provide a variety of perspectives on topics, such as migration, through the careful analysis of historical trends, individual motivations, and societal transformations. The course has the potential of offering a significant synthesis, thereby yielding cross-cultural insights into human values, attitudes, and behavior. A sample activity might involve students reading Japanese newspaper articles on illegal immigration, and making presentations to the class on Japanese perceptions of this issue.

Model III represents a new application of language study as a foundation for discipline study. It fosters the development of cultural understanding by allowing domestic and international students from a variety of language backgrounds to consider together the impact that languages have on the content of the course.

In addition to the specific curricular models designed under the grants, the 40th anniversary of the School for International Studies was seized upon as an opportunity to focus the attention of the campus on its international flavor and spotlight the international students. To that end, 1994 was declared the Year of the International Student. Special campus-wide events were inaugurated and a coordinated effort was made to have domestic students interact with international students in a more structured manner. Thus, volunteer conversation partners for international students were sought throughout the campus, and domestic students were invited to attend special EXPO nights offered by students from Showa University, Tokyo. The first course in a new undergraduate minor in Language and Linguistics was offered, and a minor in International Business was introduced. The director of Study Abroad became a full-time position, and a mandate to increase study abroad opportunities was articulated by the vice president for academic affairs.

In 1992, the undergraduate faculty had voted to amend existing course requirements to include courses with a global perspective. The Global Studies Amendment lent considerable impetus to a movement to reinstate a language requirement, which passed in 1994. In the process of implementing the language-proficiency requirement, the college established a Proficiency Office. In collaboration with the modern and classical language faculty, the Proficiency Office staff has worked to define proficiency, determine which languages will count toward proficiency, run pilot language test studies to determine the cutoff proficiency levels acceptable for the various languages, publish a proficiency newsletter, set up a summer testing and placement program, publish and distribute a "Frequently Asked Questions" brochure for students, and develop policies and procedures for accommodating students with documented learning disabilities.

In a variety of subtle and not so subtle ways, we have tried to weave an international perspective into the fabric of Saint Michael's College. Much more remains to be accomplished, but we believe that we are moving at a steady and measured pace. The above initiatives have been further buttressed by a long-range strategy of establishing linkages with educational institutions worldwide for the purpose of faculty and student exchanges, as well as cooperative programming. To date, the college has signed Memoranda of Understanding with over 20 institutions worldwide. These have already provided us with membership in the international educational community and abundant opportunities for shared learning and culturally diverse experiences for all students. In this way, internationalization will continue to flourish on the Vermont campus, as well as the worldwide campus of the global village.

Part III

LANGUAGE PROFICIENCY REVISITED

Chapter 9

Beyond Accidental Tourism: The Case for a Junior Year Abroad

Denise Rochat and Margaret Skiles Zelljadt

For 70 years, Smith College has been committed to international education through the year-long study abroad programs that it sponsors. Our programs are not reserved for a select few. On the contrary, they are designed for all qualified students committed to taking the risk of adapting as fully as possible to another culture, linguistically, academically, and socially.

The first Smith Junior Year Abroad Program was founded in Paris in 1926, and today we have three additional academic-year programs in Florence, Geneva, and Hamburg. Non-Smith students constitute 17 percent of program participants. Approximately 30 percent of all students at Smith study abroad anywhere in the world for a summer, a semester, or a year in programs that are approved by the college; 40 percent of these, or about 70 students a year, participate in our year-long programs. This paper will consider exclusively our study abroad programs in Western Europe, and specifically the two for which the authors have served as resident faculty directors; namely the program in Geneva, founded in 1946 at the Université de Genève, and the one in Hamburg, founded in 1962 at the Universtät Hamburg.

WHY STUDY ABROAD?

In the United States, reasons for advocating study abroad range from the very basic to the more substantial. There is the assumption that "any exposure to a foreign environment during one's formal education is better than none" (Goodwin and Nacht 1988, 12), or the popular rationale that significant improvement of fluency comes only through use of the foreign language in the genuine environment or the hope that time spent abroad will contribute to the development of an internationally aware citizenry. While these reasons are all valid, we justify the mandatory year's length of our study abroad programs out of a conviction that students should be provided with this unique potential for intellectual and personal development and growth. When participants in our programs cross borders, they also should become capable of crossing cultures. The student's experience should provide the opportunity for a "personal pilgrimage from ethnocentrism to ethnorelativism" (Lambert 1994, 311), a "change from a *monocultural* to an *intercultural* frame of reference" (Adler 1975, 20).

Ethnocentrism assumes that "the world view of one's own culture is central to all reality" (Bennett 1986, 33), whereas ethnorelativism posits that "cultures can only be understood *relative to one another*" (46). Anyone who has been abroad, or even in unfamiliar surroundings, has experienced what is commonly called culture shock. It has been called "the occupational hazard of overseas living through which one has to be willing to go in order to have the pleasures of experiencing other countries and cultures in depth" (Kohls 1984, 63). The adaptation process requires competence in the language of the host country and an environment conducive to cultural development. In our opinion, the primary *raison d'être* for our study abroad programs in Western Europe is to provide the appropriate framework for this personal, cultural, and intellectual experience. Subsequent sections of this chapter will address the following five components intrinsic to this enterprise:

- an academic-year program (as opposed to one lasting merely a summer or a semester);
- proficiency in the language of the host country;
- direct enrollment and virtually full integration at the host university;
- the on-site presence of a Smith faculty member who is fluent in the language and familiar with the higher education system;
- the opportunity to hold a challenging internship in the host city.

ACADEMIC YEAR ABROAD

Smith College is not alone in advocating the year-long format with full integration. In 1988, the Council for International Educational Exchange's Advisory Council claimed that "full-year programs, especially when integrated into host universities, are best of all" (Roeloffs 1994, 25). Koester also found (1985, 60) that students who had been abroad for three to 12 months showed an "increased interest in academic performance and political awareness" and that "students who directly enrolled in a foreign institution . . . established more intercultural relationships, became more politically aware, and increased their self-confidence."

One could argue that a whole year abroad is perhaps not for everyone. Nor is it for the fainthearted. Such an experience represents a wonderful opportunity, but it is also a challenge linguistically, culturally and, of course, personally. During the first four or five months of their stay, students in the initial stages of "culture shock" will of necessity stumble upon difficulties and come to know moments of frustration, alienation, and homesickness when their beliefs, values, and identity are called into question by the unfamiliarity of their surroundings. Yet, as the months go by and they slowly begin to unpack their psychological baggage, they come to realize that this initial discomfort is a necessary key to a successful integration process, a formative experience that enables them to go far beyond accidental tourism.

LANGUAGE PROFICIENCY

What Goodwin and Nacht (1988, 15) call the "main route to cultural understanding" is, of course, linguistic competence. In the age of CNN International, the NBC SuperChannel, International MTV, and the ready availability outside the U.S. of *Time, Newsweek,* or the *International Herald Tribune,* one might be tempted to question the necessity of learning and communicating in a foreign language. Yet, even those who prepare students for international business admit "we must be able to develop an understanding of the cultures with which we want to work—we must live, study, and work and even play alongside our foreign peers, and this can only be done effectively by developing the sensitivity and awareness that comes with a real understanding of the target language" (Solaun 1994, 248). Therefore, the *sine qua non* in a study abroad program with a goal of intellectual development is the acquisition of proficiency in the language of the host country.

However, Richard D. Lambert (1994, 135) deplores that "instruction taken in the language before departure tends to be relatively low." He further bemoans (136) that many U.S. students "engage in language study abroad . . . to complete the low-end requirements on the home campus." This could not be further from what takes place at Smith College. Indeed, there are no foreign language requirements at Smith (in fact, at present there are no degree requirements—other than a major—at all). Students who study a foreign language, its literature and culture, have chosen to do so of their own free will. Those who opt to study abroad in one of our programs are therefore not only highly motivated, but also committed to acquiring sufficient linguistic preparation prior to acceptance into the program.

Our study abroad programs mandate a minimum of two years of course preparation at the college level in language, literature, and culture and an average grade of B or higher in all courses. Once abroad, more intensive language instruction commences. The orientation for the Geneva program is held in Paris, where students are placed in French families. The Hamburg orientation is held in Hamburg, and students live in the dormitory rooms they will occupy for the rest of the year. Both orientations last five to six

weeks, from the end of August until the middle of October, and take place
before the official beginning of the academic year later in October.

Classes in these orientation sessions are given exclusively in the language
of the host country and are designed specifically for program students.
Their goal is to ensure that students can integrate into the local academic
culture by the beginning of the official academic year without too much
difficulty. On average, students take three to five hours of classes per day.
Courses include grammar review, conversation with on-site training aimed
at easing the process of acculturation, and analytic summaries
(*Textwiedergabe* or *comptes rendus critiques*) of newspaper articles and other
material related to the student's major or research project. The Geneva
orientation in Paris also includes phonetics and a seminar on art and
architecture. In both programs, students are required to give an oral
presentation and write a research project on a topic of their choice. A final
examination is also given in all subjects. At the end of the orientation period,
students receive a total of two credits over and above the normal, minimal
credit requirement for the academic year. [1]

Once the academic year begins, language instruction devoted to building
and sustaining language skills is incorporated into the requirements of both
programs. In Geneva, students must take at least one language course
each semester in either stylistics, oral communication, grammar review, or
translation. In Hamburg, students must take four hours a week of grammar
review each semester, unless they have been exempted through the
university examination. Linguistic and cultural integration into the local
culture in both Geneva and Hamburg are further assured by students
residing in dormitories with regular university students. Smith students
are typically assigned a single room in a suite or a floor occupied by host
nationals and international students where French or German is the lingua
franca.

Despite the intensive language instruction, we should have no illusions
about our students' real language proficiency. During the course of just
one year, they can improve significantly, especially orally, but they cannot
possibly be expected to become native writers. Hence, the need for tutorial
assistance. In Geneva, such assistance is normally provided by the director,
who helps students correct and improve all linguistic and stylistic aspects
of their papers. In Hamburg, tutors are hired to supplement courses in the
students' majors and also assist them with their written work.

INTEGRATION INTO HOST UNIVERSITIES

Immersion in the foreign language is pointless for students without an

---

1. Program directors also organized extensive excursions, which are included in
the program fee and provide a linguistic and cultural supplement to what students
are learning in class.

academic context in the foreign culture. To this end, we insist that participants in our study abroad programs be directly enrolled at the host university. This means that they are not taking classes together as a group, but study instead alongside regular university students in courses scattered across the curriculum. These courses often include advanced seminars in which students are expected to give lengthy, formal, oral presentations in front of an audience of 20 or more and respond to questions and criticism. This kind of academic integration also ensures that the course work abroad is fully accepted into their respective majors upon return. This is no mean feat, as these two programs appeal to a wide variety of majors from the social and natural sciences as well as the humanities. In the past five years, for example, students in our programs have taken courses and received credit for major subjects as diverse as history, political science, computer science, biology, art history, and religion.

FACULTY DIRECTOR

The singular personal component in the framework necessary for students' personal development is the resident director, a Smith faculty member (accompanied, when possible, by family members) whose primary responsibilities are to function as academic mentor and administrator. Describing this daunting task, John C. O'Neal (1995, 28) writes:

It is like wearing all the hats in an institution, from those worn at the top by the president, dean, and admissions and financial officers to those worn at varying levels by academic advisors, psychological counselors, career planning staff workers, accountants, secretaries, repairmen, painters, and even janitors. An overseas program director is thus a jack [or jill] of all trades except . . . the one in which he or she has the most training and experience—teaching.

The director, who also embodies and can transmit to students a sense of ethnorelativism and who has an intercultural frame of reference, is perhaps the most important person to help students who have crossed borders to also cross cultures.

INTERNSHIPS

In the context of our changing world market economy, the experiential component provided by an internship is fast becoming an essential part of college credentials. This is confirmed by the staff of the Smith College Career Development Office, who contend in one of their many brochures that "both employers and graduate schools expect applicants to have completed one or more internships as a way to demonstrate the ability to perform well in the field." When internships take place abroad, they not only help students' linguistic, cultural, and personal integration, they also complement their liberal arts training and help them "gain competence in the global marketplace" (Hoffa and Hoffa 1996, 95). The programs in Geneva and Hamburg offer students excellent opportunities for internships in various fields. [2] In Hamburg, an internship program was initiated in 1996 by the faculty director. Students worked in a wide variety of places, including a hospital, art museum, architectural firm, multicultural educational center, bank, theater group, hotel, and television show. However, since it is too early to give more details on the Hamburg internships, the second part of this chapter will be limited to the internships in Geneva and address their impact on the internationalization of the students' liberal arts education.

Internships in Geneva

The Geneva Program, established in 1946, is in some ways unique among the four Smith junior year abroad programs. First, it has never been under the control of a language department. There are, of course, French majors who go to Geneva, but they are a minority and invariably have a double major in a social science. Second, with one recent and minor exception, Smith has remained the only program of its kind whose students are allowed to enroll at the University of Geneva.

As its official title implies, the Smith College Junior Year for International Studies is an interdepartmental program especially aimed at students whose interests lie in international relations, international political economy, development and environmental studies, economic and diplomatic history, European history, humanitarian law, sociology, psychology, comparative education, and of course, French, as well as other subjects in the humanities. Directors of the program have been Smith faculty who have come from departments as varied as Government, History, Religion, Sociology, Music, and more recently, French.

The international emphasis of the program reflects the livelihood of the city itself. Geneva is home to the European office of the United Nations and countless governmental and nongovernmental international organizations that attract people from all over the world. Switzerland does not belong to either the United Nations or the European Union and therefore maintains a neutral status, allowing Geneva to continue to be the site of many international negotiations between hostile parties.

Thus, when students move from Paris to Geneva at the end of their orientation, they discover a small but cosmopolitan city situated in a French-speaking minority enclave of a tiny central European country, with a population of only six million, but four national languages and cultures.

---

2. We do not normally award academic credit for internships undertaken as part of the junior year programs. We view the internships as valuable supplemental offerings that enhance and complement but do not replace or compete with the liberal arts academic experience.

Students then realize, perhaps more acutely than ever before, that French is not the bearer of a singular (i.e., "hexagonal") culture, but a lingua franca in its own right, a tool of cultural diversity and international understanding that opens the doors to many cultures at once. First, there is the local culture with a strong Protestant identity that has been shaped and modified over the years by the various cultures of immigrant workers, who for generations have come from their native Italy, Spain, Portugal, the ex-Yugoslavia, Lebanon, Turkey, Sri Lanka, and elsewhere, and settled in the Geneva area. Second, there is the international culture dating back to the creation of the Red Cross in the middle of the nineteenth century and the League of Nations in the 1920s. Last, but not least, is the culture of neighboring France, which borders the canton of Geneva on its north, west and south sides and is only a ten-minute bus ride from the students' main residence.

To live in Geneva and study at its university, where more than half of the student body is comprised of foreigners, is therefore to be immersed in a multicultural and multilingual world, where conflicting points of view enter into a dialogue rarely heard anywhere else. Yet, it is by way of their internships within international organizations that students gain the unique opportunity to see how this dialogue, which takes place first within the walls of academia, can be implemented in today's world of global politics and economics.

Internships in Geneva were first established in 1976, thanks in great part to the contacts of a dedicated Smith alumna and her husband, who worked at the International Labor Organization (ILO). Over the years, the total number of internships has been rather low, ranging on average between one and five, depending on the size of the group and the interests of the students. In the beginning of October 1994, however, the resident director of the program was suddenly faced with a record number of 13 requests from students who wished to undertake internships in international organizations.

This sudden jump in internship requests required immediate attention and some measure of improvisation. With the invaluable assistance of the Smith alumnae network and the unfailing dedication of our contacts from the ILO, 13 internships were secured. In the spring before departure, during the on-campus orientation in Northampton, students had been informed about the possibilities for internships in Geneva and encouraged to start preparing resumés and cover letters that would be part of their files. Once in Geneva, the director edited these letters and curriculum vitae and did intensive follow-up work with potential internship providers. When an internship materialized, the director tried to match students' interests, backgrounds, and personalities with the position. Once students had arranged their initial interviews, the director faxed dossiers to the various organizations, along with a personal letter of introduction and recommendation. In the cases where two or three students were ideally suited for one internship possibility, the director arranged to have all of them interviewed, with the hope that supervisors would be so impressed by these young people that they would not have the heart to turn them down and would find them additional positions, either in their organization or elsewhere. This is precisely what happened in two cases, where the interviews yielded a total of five internships.

Most interviews for internships took place in November and December. Students were typically asked to talk about their academic interests, explain their reasons for wanting an internship, and what they hoped to accomplish. The skills required included fluency in French and, if possible, other foreign languages; good analytical, writing, and editing skills; knowledge of word processing programs, and most importantly, a strong academic background to enable them to carry out critical research. [3]

The majority of the internships—all of them unpaid—started in January and lasted three to eight months. The schedules during the academic year tended to be very flexible. Students usually worked an average of six to 12 hours per week, either for a whole day or two half days a week. Ample accommodations were made for students during "crunch times," such as seminar presentations and semester or year-end examinations. Three of the students who continued their internships during the summer (July and August) worked full-time during that period.

In the majority of cases, French was used in conjunction with English for oral communication, correspondence, and for reading and research. Several students were fluent in Spanish, Portuguese, German, or Hungarian and also used these languages for their research and communication. Most of the writing, however, was done in English.

Once the internships got underway, the director checked with students regularly but informally to address problems as quickly as possible. In the one case where the internship turned out to be a failure (due mainly to a lack of structure and organization on the part of the supervisor), the director arranged for an amiable and acceptable termination. Towards the end of the academic year, the director invited supervisors either individually or in small groups to dinner to thank them for their past commitment and to pave the way for continued cooperation in the future.

Students' projects consisted mainly of research in the fields of development studies, international political economics, labor unions, the environment, and the international art world. One student worked at the United Nations Environment Program in the department of the

---

3. The director designed a questionnaire at the end of their senior year in which students were asked factual questions about their interview, their schedule, the duration of the internship, their supervisor, and the type of work they did. Students were also asked to address issues such as the relationship between the internship and their academic program, as well as the interaction between the culture of their international organization and that of the host university. The comments compiled for this chapter come from ten of the 13 students who responded.

International Register for Potential Toxic Chemicals, where she helped update the query and response system. Two students worked at the International Academy of the Environment: one on a project documenting how primary and secondary schools in Europe and elsewhere integrate environmental issues into their traditional curriculum; the other did extensive research on the conservation of fossil fuels—her work was eventually incorporated into her supervisor's paper, which the student also edited.

Two students interned at the International Cooperative Alliance (ICA): one read and summarized articles about cooperatives for publication in their newsletter; the other was given the opportunity to create and present her own set of guidelines for development projects designed by grassroots organizations. The International Labor Organization provided two internships: one student worked on the concept of "sustainable livelihoods," analyzed various ILO/UN projects, and evaluated their impact on the livelihoods of individuals in developing countries; the other drafted a proposal for the Philippine government concerning the country's adoption of an ILO convention on the rights of indigenous people. Her other research projects included urban and rural labor unions in Ghana, and the general need for restructuring the country's labor unions in the face of a fast-changing global economy.

Two students worked at a nongovernmental organization (NGO) for the Convention on the Rights of the Child. They researched children's rights issues, wrote reports, attended meetings at the United Nations, took notes, and wrote summaries of UN documents. They also wrote articles for the *Defense for Children International Newsletter*. One of them was assigned a research project on the relationship between NGOs and the United Nations, to be published the following year.

Finally, at Christie's, one student was assigned to the jewelry department where she helped organize two big annual sales. She also researched and wrote biographies of women jewelry designers, which were included in the sale catalogs.

In most instances, the internships proved to be academically and intellectually relevant to a liberal arts education. The students, in general, were convinced the internship contributed significantly to their research, analytic, and writing skills. Almost all said that they were able to apply their previous academic knowledge to their internship work. Many also drew upon what they had learned during their internships for course work in the senior year. One student, for example, took a development course and used the research she did at the ICA for a comparative study on development. Two others students created independent studies based on research associated with their internship. Virtually all of them confirmed that they had gained new, broader, and more concrete insights into international issues. As a result, one student was reaffirmed in her wish to study international law at the graduate level, two others realized that their true calling was in the field of international development, while a fourth student said that her "internship was vital and formative," helping her to focus her career on "human rights within the foreign policy arena."

It is too early to speak about the precise impact these internships will have on the students' professional and academic careers. If current results are any indication, however, the impact will be significant. Of the 13 students who had internships, three returned to their internship organizations the following summer, and three others returned to Geneva in the fall of 1996 to enroll in doctoral programs at the Graduate Institute of International Relations.

While students were keenly aware of the culture of the international organizations, they experienced no secondary culture shock. Instead, they found that the organizational culture simply mirrored the highly international culture of Geneva and its university. While initially they were shocked by the many bureaucratic inefficiencies of the UN and its affiliated organizations, as they grew more involved with their projects and came to know and respect their supervisors, they realized that behind the political feuding are many hardworking, dedicated people who form the backbone of this institution. In many cases, these supervisors took a genuine interest in our students and even acted as mentors. Thanks to these supervisors' dedication and willingness to provide the right balance of autonomy and intellectual support, these young people were able to reflect on international issues in a truly global context. As a result, many of our students were inspired or strengthened in their desire and commitment to work further within the international field.

All of our collective efforts at helping students acquire sufficient language proficiency to study successfully at a foreign university and partake of the work culture abroad are for naught if we cannot sustain the program enrollments and enjoy an ongoing dialogue with administrators and faculty in support of the programs. The programs abroad must be assured of continued financial support, particularly in years where numbers are lean and/or exchange rates are to our disadvantage. As faculty members, we realize that the support of colleagues in non-language departments is essential in making a year abroad part of the overall Smith experience. Study in a foreign country offers students the potential for academic and personal growth that is unparalleled on the home campus. The year abroad simply cannot be measured merely in terms of courses and credits.

All institutions with study abroad programs are facing a very real dilemma brought on by decreasing enrollments and increasing budgets. A frequently suggested way out of this dilemma is to lower foreign language prerequisites or reduce the amount of time students must spend abroad, thus potentially making study abroad programs available to more students. The authors, having been directors abroad, believe neither of these solutions is acceptable. In either case, the basic nature and intrinsic goals of our study abroad programs would be compromised. Instead, the programs must have affirmation at every level of the institution.

Our most important and valuable resource, however, will always be our students. Approximately half of the students in our programs claimed they chose Smith because of our opportunities for study abroad. When they return as seniors, their voices speak loudest and most convincingly in favor of maintaining study abroad programs in their present form. One student has called the year abroad "a year full of discovery and challenge"; another termed it "an eye-opening experience as far as languages and cultures are concerned"; and a third declared it to be "the most intense year in my life—personally and academically." Virtually all of them maintained that the year abroad was the most important in terms of enriching their overall liberal arts education.

REFERENCES

Adler, Peter S. 1975. "The Transitional Experience: An Alternative View of Culture Shock." *The Journal of Humanistic Psychology* 15, no. 4 (fall): 13-23.

Bennett, Milton J. 1986. "Towards Ethnorelativism: A Development Model of Intercultural Sensitivity." *Cross-Cultural Orientation: New Conceptualizations and Applications*. Edited by R. Michael Paige, 27-69. Lanham, Md.: University Press of America.

Goodwin, Craufurd D. and Michael Nacht. 1988. *Abroad and Beyond: Patterns in American Overseas Education*. Cambridge, Mass.: Cambridge University Press.

Hoffa, Bill and Rosalind Hoffa. 1996. "Helping Students Plan: Study Abroad and International Careers." *Transitions Abroad* (March/April): 94-96.

Koester, Jolene. 1985. *A Profile of the U.S. Student Abroad*. New York: Council on International Educational Exchange.

Kohls, L. Robert. 1984. *Survival Kit for Overseas Living*. Yarmouth, Maine: Intercultural Press, Inc.

Lambert, Richard D. 1994. "Some Issues in Language Policy for Higher Education." *Annals of the American Academy of Political and Social Sciences* 532 (March): 123-137.

O'Neal, John C. 1995. "It's Like Wearing All the Hats." *Academe* (September/October): 28-34.

Roeloffs, Karl. 1994. "Global Competence and Regional Integration: A View from Europe." *Educational Exchange and Global Competence*. Edited by Richard D. Lambert, 25-36. New York: Council on International Educational Exchange.

Solaun, Joan D. 1994. "Language Acquisition and Study Abroad: What Do We Want to Accomplish?" *Educational Exchange and Global Competence*. Edited by Richard D. Lambert, 247-254. New York: Council on International Educational Exchange.

Chapter 10

Foreign Languages Across the Curriculum at Home and Abroad

Merle Krueger

The drive to internationalize higher education in the United States has hit a serious snag. The 1979 report of President Carter's Commission on Foreign Language and International Studies deplored Americans' "scandalous" incompetency in foreign languages and warned that our future as a global leader was imperiled by our widespread ignorance of international affairs. In response to the conclusions reached in this and subsequent reports by government and academic task forces, policymakers and education leaders launched initiatives to internationalize the curriculum in the nation's colleges and universities. Now that institutions of higher learning throughout the country have embraced this aim, powerful forces in Congress have begun to withdraw government support. Appealing to deeply entrenched isolationist traditions, these politicians would have us retreat behind a "fortress America" mentality. On the foreign policy level, this plays out in moves to withhold dues from international organizations such as the United Nations or to sharply reduce foreign aid, while on the domestic education front it becomes manifest in calls to cut bilingual education or the Fulbright exchange programs.

Yet, the importance of cultivating an international perspective among the American public has never been more vital. Not only does economic interdependence among nations challenge the United States to boost our competitiveness in a global marketplace, virtually every aspect of our security and quality of life requires a response to developments throughout the Earth. Advocates of international studies can point to constantly shifting strategic concerns in the post-Cold War era, where threats to peace and security no longer coalesce along a clear ideological fault line, but instead present a highly fractured and diffuse image. Ecological dangers and public health risks are leapfrogging continental boundaries; communication and information technologies are expanding exponentially throughout the world; demographic shifts and emigration patterns are redistributing populations across borders; a world popular culture is emerging—these and other developments are reinforcing an evolving planetary consciousness. More than ever, our national interests require an educated citizenry that appreciates both the global context and implications of our policy decisions. Higher education must respond by nurturing awareness that our individual welfare depends ineluctably upon the fate of the Earth as a whole.

The study of languages is essential to this educational process. The essence of another culture is embedded in its language and cannot be probed or comprehended with much subtlety without knowledge of the language in which it expresses itself. At the same time, studying another culture is perhaps the best way to understand and appreciate what is unique about our own culture and social traditions. Goethe once wrote: "Whoever does not know a foreign language does not know his own," and what is true of language in this sense, is true of culture and civilization in general. Arguably, however, relatively little is gained by only a few semesters of study in a language, which is then dropped after the general education requirement is met. The former director of the National Foreign Language Center, Richard Lambert, once described language study in the United States as, "a mile wide and an inch deep." Many colleges and universities have retained or reinstated a foreign language requirement, but stipulating completion of three or four courses for graduation does not hold much promise for deepening language competency to the point where students can use the language effectively for professional purposes.

Americans generally tend to grossly underestimate how much effort it takes to learn a second language well. Learning our mother tongue comes naturally; virtually everyone masters the complexities of grammar and semantics in their first language at an early age. But mastering a second or third language typically takes years of intense study, and even after decades of practice, few people attain true native-like proficiency. According to data collected and analyzed by the School of Language Studies of the Foreign Service Institute (FSI), American students with a superior aptitude for languages typically require 720 hours of classroom instruction to reach Level 3 in oral skills in French or Spanish. [1] Level 3 (on the government FSI oral proficiency scale) is defined as, "able to speak the language with sufficient structural accuracy and vocabulary to participate effectively in most formal and informal conversations." If we assume that students receive 90 hours of classroom instruction in a typical semester-long course, then according to the above it would require eight semesters to attain a Level 3 oral proficiency in French and Spanish—a proficiency level, be it

---

1. See Alice C. Omaggio, *Teaching Language in Context: Proficiency-Oriented Instruction*, Boston: Heinle and Heinle, 1986, p. 19 ff.

noted, far from near-native! For languages such as Arabic and Chinese, which fall into the most difficult category for native-English speakers, the comparable number of classroom hours of instruction falls between 2,400 and 2,760—the equivalent of 27 to 31 semesters!

LINKING LANGUAGE STUDY TO OTHER DISCIPLINES

In light of the time it takes, how can our students ever acquire genuine communicative competence in other languages? The answer to this question is complex and multifaceted. Surely, part of the answer lies in starting language instruction at an earlier age in our primary and secondary schools, and improving the so-called "articulation" or curricular coordination between levels and schools. Another part of the answer is to encourage students to continue their study of the language beyond the requirement for graduation and the third or fourth semester level, which represents merely a threshold to true proficiency. Enrolling in upper division literature courses, perhaps even pursuing a double major in a language along with another discipline may be an option for some students. Extended study abroad is another viable alternative, especially when participants undertake academic work and interact with native speakers using the language.

Brown University and a growing number of other institutions have been pursuing another option, linking language study and use with course work in disciplines across the curriculum. [2] The rationale behind this innovation, known at Brown as "foreign language across the curriculum" (FLAC), resembles the thinking behind earlier "writing across the curriculum" ventures. Instructors of college writing courses reasoned that since the skill of writing is integral to all academic work, the study of writing should not be limited to composing essays within English departments. In most American colleges and universities, students who wish to pursue study of a language beyond the intermediate level have little choice but to enroll in literature or culture courses. FLAC recognizes that individuals may wish to use their second language in a wide variety of fields; that, in fact, the analysis of material from another cultural perspective and in another language, significantly enriches one's understanding of a topic. The idea is to encourage students to use their second language abilities in areas that interest them, to discover in the process that a second language has genuine value in their field, and to develop the habit of applying their language skills regularly as a key to learning. Ideally, students will consult second language sources for their other courses, too, and eventually will view their language skills as an integral component of their professional and personal lives.

Under the direction of the Center for Language Studies, since the early

2. See Merle Krueger and Frank Ryan, eds., *Language and Content: Discipline- and Content-Based Approaches in Language Study*, Lexington, Mass.: D. C. Heath, 1993.

1990s Brown University has adapted a number of courses for its FLAC program, supported financially by grants from Title VI of the Department of Education, the Fund for the Improvement of Post-Secondary Education, and the Ford Foundation. To date, 19 courses have been developed and taught by members of the departments of French Studies, Comparative Literature, History, Afro-American Studies, Italian Studies, Latin American Studies, German Studies, Slavic Languages, Anthropology, International Relations, East Asian Studies, Art and Architecture, and Political Science, and including the following languages: Arabic, Chinese, French, German, Hebrew, Italian, Japanese, Portuguese, Russian, and Spanish.

FLAC courses at Brown follow several models. The most common format involves a regular lecture course conducted in English paired with a separate language section, taught by the course professor or a graduate student. In this FLAC section, most or all of the activities (discussions, readings, video or film showings, writing assignments) are carried out in the target language. These sections are open to all interested students who possess sufficient command of the language, subject to approval of the instructor. No extra credit is given for participation in a FLAC section of a course, although in some cases work done in the second language may be substituted for readings or other course assignments in English. Sometimes a FLAC section is team-taught by the course instructor together with a language department instructor, and in a few cases the entire course has been conducted in the foreign language.

FLAC AS PREPARATION FOR STUDY ABROAD

The following pages describe two separate FLAC courses at Brown with particular relevance for study abroad, the first in French and the second in Italian. Study abroad logically extends the "foreign language across the curriculum" concept, notably in those programs where students enroll in regular courses at the host university alongside their native-speaking peers. For these study abroad participants, the second language serves as the medium for learning course content, as in a FLAC section. But of course the differences are significant, too. In those study abroad programs where American students attend regular university lectures and seminars, the linguistic challenges are likely to be greater than in a FLAC course, for the professor will present the material in an academic register and at a tempo appropriate to highly educated adult native speakers. In a FLAC section, most, if not all of the participants, will be learners of the language who experience some difficulties with it, at least occasionally. In a regular university course abroad, the American students will be in a linguistic minority. Few will have the language proficiency and self-confidence not to feel intimidated; most will be downright overwhelmed, at least in the beginning.

Do the benefits justify the effort required? And how do we maximize the benefits? Language educators recognize the potential gains in proficiency of extended immersion in the target language community. Yet, study abroad itself does not automatically lead to substantial language improvement. A number of factors seem to be involved in determining how effectively study abroad produces linguistic gains, including length of stay, individual foreign language aptitude, motivation, learning strategies, prior background in the target language, even gender. [3] Research in second language acquisition during study abroad indicates that, not surprisingly, language improvement seems contingent upon the amount and kinds of interactions conducted with native speakers in the target language. Those who are constantly struggling to negotiate meanings in the language generally make greater strides than those who lack or avoid such opportunities.

There is little conclusive research evidence to determine the impact of the formal instructional context on language acquisition abroad. This goes for both formal language instruction per se and for instruction in other disciplines conducted in the target language. The lack of substantiated information on these matters no doubt derives in part from the difficulties of identifying and isolating the many significant variables involved. However, if we concur with Stephen Krashen's input hypothesis that second language acquisition depends on the amount of comprehensible input the student receives, it seems reasonable to conclude that language gains will be minimal in formal lectures and seminars where the students comprehend little or nothing of what's going on.

Faculty at Brown University have designed two language courses as part of the FLAC program which aim to help prepare students for the rigorous linguistic demands of regular university study abroad. "French for International Relations" (French 51) is intended for social science concentrators, especially political science and international relations majors, who plan to study at the Institut D'Études Politiques, a prestigious institute of political science in Paris. "Introduction to Italian Culture" (Italian 90A) is taught during the orientation period of the year-long Brown-in-Bologna program. In general terms, the objective is to improve students' proficiency in all four language modes (listening, speaking, reading, writing), as well as specifically to prepare students as quickly as possible for course work alongside native Italian students at the University of Bologna.

Both courses employ a "content-based" (or "discipline-based") approach to language study, the pedagogical principle underlying the entire "foreign language across the curriculum" initiative. Simply put, a content- or discipline-based approach stresses the use of language for learning subject

---

3. For an overview of research on language acquisition and study abroad, see Thom Huebner. "A Framework for Investigating the Effectiveness of Study Abroad." *Redefining the Boundaries of Language Study*. Edited by Claire Kramsch. Boston: Heinle and Heinle, 1995, 185-217.

matter in a given field or discipline. Rather than concentrating attention primarily on the language itself as a syntactic and semantic system, content-based instruction emphasizes comprehension of the information and ideas (the "content") which the language conveys. Some attention is devoted to grammatical constructions, but within a context of the expression of meaning in a text. Students are engaged in the negotiation of meaning. Improved language proficiency derives from using the language to learn.

In a policy statement, *What We Can't Say Can Hurt Us: A Call for Foreign Language Competence by the Year 2000*, the American Council on Education recommended that U.S. colleges and universities "provide opportunities for students in all disciplines and preprofessional programs to achieve high levels of foreign language proficiency by a combination of preparatory courses, intensive courses, and foreign study and internships, as well as the infusion of international and foreign language materials into substantive disciplinary courses" (1989, 3). The two language courses described below address elements in this recommendation. Together they suggest the outlines of a comprehensive curriculum reform which might bring us considerably closer to the goal that "all students in all disciplines ... achieve high levels of foreign language proficiency."

"FRENCH FOR INTERNATIONAL RELATIONS"

With support from a Title VI grant from the U.S. Department of Education awarded in fall 1990, Professor François Hugot completely rewrote the syllabus for fifth semester French, so that in addition to the more traditional "Writing and Speaking French II" students now have the option of a class entitled "French for International Relations." International relations is the most popular concentration among Brown undergraduates, and many international relations students elect to study abroad in France during their junior year. Especially appealing for them among the destinations in France is the Institut d'Études Politiques de Paris, a highly select, world-renowned institution for political science, known by its nickname "Sciences Po." Professor Hugot conceived his course for social science students, particularly international relations and political science concentrators with plans to study in France. He devoted part of the course specifically for preparing students to pass the notoriously rigorous French entrance exam at Sciences Po. "French for International Relations" provides instruction in all language modes, while focusing on the specialized discourse of international relations in French. Scholarly texts used in the course span all four major divisions of the international relations concentration at Brown: (1) diplomacy and foreign policy; (2) international peace and security; (3) north/south relations; and (4) international commerce.

Professor Hugot organized the course in an innovative way. Class time, three 50-minute sessions per week, was spent almost exclusively on practicing oral discourse, including large and small group discussions, oral reports on specified topics, presentations by the professor on "the functioning of the language" (problems of syntax or the pragmatics of discourse), or an alternative activity. Students were also expected to do a substantial amount of work outside class. The makeup of these tasks was highly individualized. In an attempt to address each person's particular needs as much as possible, students negotiated a contract with the professor at the outset of the course, with opportunities periodically throughout the semester for review and revision of its provisions. The contracts stipulated the kinds and amount of out-of-class assignments they promised to complete, with attention concentrated on reading, listening/speaking, or writing, depending on the students' self-assessments of the skill areas in which they needed the most work.

To improve listening/speaking proficiency, class participants viewed French news broadcasts in the Language Resource Center at specified hours. French language films and videotapes were also available in the lab. Native French undergraduate teaching assistants watched these segments along with them and acted as discussion partners, explaining difficult concepts or cultural references. These teaching assistants were recruited among students studying at Brown under the auspices of the university's exchange agreements with French universities, and were selected on the basis of their knowledge of international relations. They also served as discussion leaders for special small-group sessions devoted to readings on specialized topics. Class members could also consult with the assistants for help composing essays and term papers in French.

Professor Hugot compiled a large list of reading materials, including scholarly books, journal articles, and newspaper articles (from *Le Monde*, *Liberation*, and others). Among the required readings were selections from "classic" works in the fields of international relations and political science, and newspaper and magazine articles dealing with current events. Those in the class who felt they needed extra work in reading were assigned additional titles from the list.

Students were required to complete a variety of writing tasks as well, using computer software specially designed by Professor Hugot called "Ateliers d'Écriture." Introductory assignments to write a letter, diary, story, and essay provided opportunities to practice composition while enhancing awareness of genre conventions. Subsequent writing assignments in the specialized discourse of the discipline included writing a narrative paraphrase and an explication of an argument developed by someone else, a critical report of an article or book section, and an essay.

The course also featured special activities and individual projects. As mentioned above, one of the course objectives was to prepare students to pass the French entrance exam for foreign students at the Institut d'Études Politiques. Actual exams from previous years were adapted for writing practice. The examination typically includes the following tasks: (1) write a summary of a short text on a topic pertinent to the discipline; (2) explain some formulations or expressions in the text; (3) explicate an aspect of the author's argument; and (4) write a brief essay on an assigned (related) topic.

Another special project, the so-called *Tables Rondes*, organized large group discussions on a major topic in international relations. Professor Hugot suggested three topics (European unification, peace and security, north/south relations) and compiled for each a dossier containing a bibliography of articles and books available in the university library. Once the students collectively decided upon a topic, each agreed to read two titles on a particular subtopic. Over a two-week preparation period, the students were responsible for analyzing the readings and identifying the specific points of view of the authors. In the process, they were encouraged to consult with the French teaching assistants in order to comprehend difficult points or arguments, and to assess the ideological position of the writers, often an especially difficult task for second language learners since it requires them to make inferences from presuppositions and attend to subtleties of expression such as irony or humor. Two class periods were then devoted to the *Table Rondes*; during the first, each student had five minutes to present his or her subtopic, while in the second, a group discussion of the general topic took place.

Finally, special individual projects could also be contracted in order to accommodate a special interest or strengthen a special skill. For example, one student combined listening comprehension, speaking, and writing by interviewing a number of Francophone students and faculty on campus. Her project investigated these individuals' perceptions of German reunification and their reactions to it. She taped the conversations, transcribed them, and then wrote evaluative analyses of the data.

The contract system employed in the course provided each student with a weekly critique and assessment of his or her work throughout the semester, and this made a final examination unnecessary. In their evaluations, participants have praised the approach of integrating French language instruction with subject matter from international relations and political science. The first year, "French for International Relations" attracted an enrollment of seven students, whereupon its reputation spread quickly among international relations students. By the next fall, 20 students had enrolled. Following Professor Hugot's retirement, the course continued to be offered in the Department of French Studies and remains popular among undergraduates in the social sciences.

BROWN-IN-BOLOGNA PROGRAM

American study abroad programs are generally of two types, so-called "island programs" where U.S. students receive instruction in separate courses designed exclusively for them, and programs which expect students to enroll in regular courses at the host institution alongside their native-speaking counterparts. Programs of the "island" variety deal with the linguistic challenges of college-level course work in a foreign language, either by simplifying the language of instruction in sheltered classes for foreign students, or by avoiding the issue altogether, offering all or most of their classes in English. Programs which mainstream students into standard university courses taught in the language commonly adopt a "sink or swim" attitude. Students are expected to try their best to keep up with their native-speaking peers, do the readings, attend the lectures and take notes, write required term papers, participate in group discussions, and take tests. Only a small minority can achieve this feat in their first semester abroad; most flounder and learn little actual content or language in their courses. At best, some programs of this type arrange for tutors to help the students struggle through as well as they can.

A third type of study abroad program combines aspects of the other two. Intensive language courses exclusively for the foreign students are given during presemester orientation or in the first semester of the year, and thereafter students are expected to take some or all of their courses from the host university curriculum. This arrangement is designed to ease the transition into the demanding atmosphere of lectures and seminars that are conducted in an idiom appropriate for highly educated adult native speakers.

The Brown-in-Bologna Program is an example of this third type, with an intensive nine-week-long Italian language course taught during presemester orientation in early fall. All program participants are required to enroll in the course, which has been designed by Dedda DeAngelis, senior lecturer in Brown's Italian Studies Department, specifically to prepare students for regular courses at the University of Bologna in late October. The syllabus employs principles of content-based instruction and emphasizes comprehension of the informational content of a given language text, rather than analysis of its syntactic structure. Above all, this is achieved by linking the Italian language course to a separate required course in contemporary Italian history and culture, much in the way a FLAC course connects language study with another academic discipline.

The language course in Bologna is divided into three sections that meet for either six or eight hours per week for nine weeks, depending on the proficiency level of the student. The sections that meet more frequently are intended for those less solidly prepared in the language, i.e., the intermediate and low-intermediate students. All students in the program are required to enroll simultaneously in the nine-week history course, which focuses more on either contemporary social and political history, or contemporary cultural history and civilization, depending on who teaches it in a given year. Although it is an "island" course, exclusively for the Brown-in-Bologna students, the history course is taught much like a regular Italian university course, in a lecture format with substantial reading assignments and little classroom discussion.

Consistent with a content-based approach, all three sections of the Italian language course are geared to a significant degree towards the subject matter in the history course. The two intensive language sections devote half the time to a general review of grammar and syntax according to a "functionally organized" syllabus. This part of the course aims to build students' communicative competence in all four skills, with situations relevant to their academic and nonacademic experiences in Bologna. In these two sections, the other half of class time (and in the third more advanced section, the entire course) is dedicated to the study of the Italian language in linkage with the study of contemporary Italian history or culture. Class discussions deal with the material currently being covered in the history lectures and assigned readings. Students' oral practice relies heavily on their notes of the lectures. Video and film are also employed in the two parallel courses; especially authentic documentary footage, for example, of a speech by Mussolini.

Two term papers are assigned in the history course (one 15 pages in length, due midterm, and a 20-page final paper), which they must first submit in draft form in the language course. The language instructor examines and comments upon the formal features of these papers, their syntax, vocabulary choices, style, and discourse aspects, but —as far as it is possible to separate the two—not on the papers' substance; that is, the arguments the students develop, the evidence they muster to support these points, and the accuracy of their judgments on the historical subject matter. Ms. DeAngelis points out that the language teachers identify, but do not correct students' mistakes, nor do they grade the papers. Students are responsible for rewriting a final draft for submission to their history instructor, who alone affixes a grade on the overall quality of the finished paper.

It would be misleading to imply that the content-based approach to language instruction ignores consideration of grammar and linguistic form. Specific aspects of Italian grammar are examined, but within the larger context posed by the content being learned. For this part of the course, the progression of themes and topics in the history course drives the syllabus. Specific attention is devoted to aspects of the discourse of history as an academic discipline; for example, the widespread use of impersonal *si* constructions and the tendency towards hypotaxis and interwoven dependent clause constructions.

The large amounts of reading of academic texts required in regular university courses pose particular difficulties for the less-proficient students in Bologna. In order to rapidly improve the reading skills of these students, Ms. DeAngelis has compiled a special workbook of exercises for the early weeks of the language course in the intensive sections. In both versions of the history course, students are required to read a collection of lectures on Italian fascism, entitled *L'Italia Contemporanea*, delivered originally at the Sorbonne by the historian Chabod. The volume causes newly arrived students many problems beyond the general shock of reading a work of scholarship in Italian for the first time. For one thing, it presupposes considerable familiarity with figures and events of the fascist era. Unlike standard history textbooks, the style tends towards the essayistic, with a line of argumentation not strictly expository and chronological, but drawing inferences, connections, and deductions of a conceptual nature. Add to this a scholarly vocabulary and lengthy and involved syntactical structures, and the low-intermediate and intermediate students invariably feel overwhelmed.

The workbook, *Esercizi per la Lettura del Testo: Chabod: L'Italia Contemporanea*, compiles a set of exercises for each segment of the text assigned for reading in the history course. A list of vocabulary items with their specific English equivalents in the context aims to reduce the time students need to consult their dictionaries, so they can get through the segment somewhat faster. Next, one or two concise sentences summarize the main concepts or ideas in each paragraph, providing a means for students to check whether they comprehended the gist of that passage. Arrows designate names of important historical figures or events which they should be able to identify or define; this may mean consulting an encyclopedia or other reference work. Several exercises on the reading follow that reinforce vocabulary items, syntactic structures, and historical identifications or definitions. These may include fill-in-the-blank questions, verb tense changes or inflections, and phrase-, sentence-, or short paragraph-length answers. The farther along one proceeds in the workbook, the shorter the supports to comprehension become (vocabulary lists and summarizing sentences).

The workbook exercises, classroom activities, term papers, and other homework assigned and discussed in the language course reinforce comprehension of the material presented in the history lectures and readings. It is important to note that the content of the history course is thus approached from several angles. The facts and concepts presented in the course on contemporary Italian history and culture are in effect reiterated and recycled in the language course. The same specific historical event may serve as the context for discussion practice, exercises in vocabulary recognition or reflexive verb constructions, and academic writing tasks. Progress in learning the language accompanies progress in learning history. Students absorb knowledge of the academic discipline of history at the same time that they deepen their proficiency in Italian.

Students in the Bologna Program credit the content-based approach of their language course and its link to the contemporary Italian history course with enabling them to progress quickly in reading Italian academic texts. They also make rapid strides in comprehending lectures in Italian, and show marked improvement in the quality of their written work. Naturally, as with any approach and any subject, not all students demonstrate the same rate of improvement, but by the end of the year in Italy, almost all the program participants are performing well in their regular courses at the University of Bologna. The paired history/language courses in the orientation period seem successful in preparing even marginally proficient students to handle substantive academic work in Italian alongside their Italian peers.

More than ever, the study of a second language to the point of genuine proficiency is a vital element of a liberal arts education, for lack of such ability limits our cross-cultural awareness in a time of rapidly increasing global interdependence. We must not underestimate the substantial effort required to achieve communicative competence. It is unfair to students to convey the impression that four semesters worth of language study, or the equivalent, is sufficient to prepare them to use a second language in their professional careers. We should not expect college students merely to complete a certain requirement, only to drop the language entirely after graduation, and never use it again to read a single article or engage in a single conversation.

New curricular configurations are necessary which encourage students to pursue their study of languages beyond the fourth semester level, which represents, at best, a threshold to true proficiency. Undergraduates should become accustomed to integrating second language use in their study of other academic disciplines. FLAC programs such as those at Brown University and elsewhere suggest how this might work, though the variety of second language activities and the number and kinds of courses with second language components need to be greatly expanded. More students from more disciplines need to study for longer periods in more venues abroad, and their learning experiences there, including language, need increased rigor and smoother coordination within their overall undergraduate careers. Perhaps the two examples of innovative language courses outlined above will stimulate further initiatives in this direction.

REFERENCES

American Council of Education. 1989. *What We Can't Say Can Hurt Us: A Call for Foreign Language Competence by the Year 2000*. Washington, D.C.
President's Commission on Foreign Language and International Studies. 1979. *Strength through Wisdom: A Critique of U.S. Capability. A Report to the President from the President's Commission on Foreign Language and International Studies*. Washington, D.C.: U.S. Government Printing Office.

Part IV

BREAKING WITH TRADITION: NEW CONTEXTS, NEW APPROACHES

Chapter 11

From Serendipity to Strategy: International Education Across the Curriculum

Michael Kline and Neil Weissman

Most American colleges and universities recognize the need for an international dimension in undergraduate education. At least some understanding of the world beyond the borders of the United States invariably finds its place among the criteria determining curriculum. At the same time, commitment to international education is usually expressed in piecemeal fashion. A requirement in foreign language or world culture, majors in language and an area study or two, an off-campus study office, perhaps with an abroad program sponsored by the institution itself—all without much coordination or integration—are often assumed to do the trick.

This characterization would certainly have applied to Dickinson College's international education program before the 1980s. The college had maintained a foreign language requirement since its eighteenth-century founding. Indeed, in the early 1970s, an agreement by the language departments to have an intensive, five contact-hour per week language requirement in return for a 15-student limit on class size meant that foreign language specialists accounted for one-fifth of the faculty. In addition, social science faculty had established an overseas program in Bologna, Italy and even joined with the language departments to offer Russian Area and International Studies majors. Yet, this relative depth in international education was more fortuitous than the result of any institutional plan.

During the 1980s, the college essentially moved from serendipity to strategy in international programming. The catalyst for a more systematic approach was a pair of grants from the National Endowment for the Humanities (NEH): the first, an Excellence in a Field Grant of $300,000 to develop international education; and the second a $1 million Challenge Grant to endow what was accomplished. The result has been a program distinguished not only by its depth, but also, we believe, by its reach across the campus and degree of integration.

The college's international education program is perhaps best conceived in terms of concentric circles (see Figure 11.1). At the core are strong majors in foreign language and literature. The college offers instruction in 11 languages, and just under one-fifth of our students major in foreign language. This exceptional vitality of foreign language study has many sources, ranging from the significant staff cohort to active recruitment by the college's admissions staff. The chief motor in the growth of language study—and of globalization in general—has been the development of study centers abroad.

Figure 11.1
International Education at Dickinson: A Conceptual Model

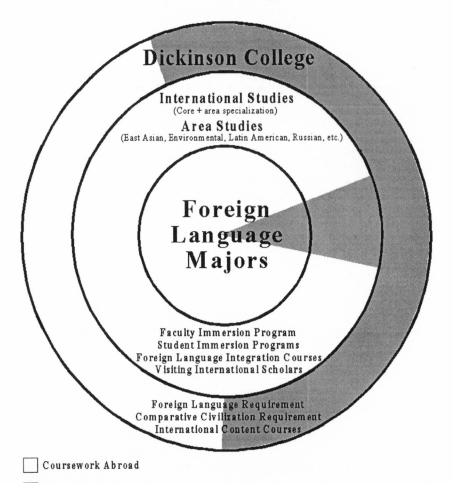

Dickinson College

International Studies
(Core + area specialization)
Area Studies
(East Asian, Environmental, Latin American, Russian, etc.)

Foreign
Language
Majors

Faculty Immersion Program
Student Immersion Programs
Foreign Language Integration Courses
Visiting International Scholars

Foreign Language Requirement
Comparative Civilization Requirement
International Content Courses

☐ Coursework Abroad

▨ No Coursework Abroad

OVERSEAS STUDY CENTERS ARE KEY

More than any other component of transformation, our overseas programs have contributed to an ethos on the campus that promotes global awareness, raises academic expectations, and promotes recruiting. Before 1985, Dickinson's only wholly-owned program was located in Bologna, having its primary emphasis in the social sciences, particularly political science and international relations. Students desiring to study elsewhere were sent to programs affiliated with the college. Although, as a constituent member of these programs, Dickinson had a voice in decision making, we were not always satisfied with the level of course work, the supervision of our students, and particularly the articulation between courses taken on campus before departure, during the study abroad experience, and the senior year on the campus.

Our desire to become totally responsible for predeparture preparation, the abroad experience itself, and students' reintegration, motivated the opening of Dickinson's first Study Center abroad, in Toulouse, France, in 1985. This center was followed by ones in Málaga, Spain and Bremen, Germany. Others followed shortly (see Figure 11.2). In addition to the semester/year programs, several of the centers developed intensive summer immersion programs in language and civilization. Intended for students at the intermediate level of language development, these immersions are simultaneously a capstone experience for students completing the language requirement and a bridge for those continuing toward more advanced levels.

Each of the programs abroad has its own character, which is a reflection both of Dickinson's pluralistic community and the varying aspirations we have for students, as demonstrated in the goals of the different programs and departments. Some sites own property, others rent or lease it. Some larger sites have a Dickinson director in residence, while others rely on a resident university colleague in the college's part-time employ. At many sites students live with families. Most centers teach courses that have been conceptualized on the home campus with smooth articulation between the American and foreign curriculum in mind, while most offer the opportunity for the student to integrate into various university schools and institutes, as well. Internships are possible at a number of sites. Today, our constellation of study abroad sites is nearly complete. We are thinking about a new center in Latin America, as well as the Pacific or North Africa.

PORTABLE FINANCIAL AID

The multiplication of opportunities to study abroad has not only become a huge extension to Dickinson's campus of 1,800 students, but it is also the source of constant opportunity and challenge. A key decision to make financial aid portable was made early on. Dickinson students who are enrolled in Dickinson programs abroad may take their financial aid with

Figure 11.2
Dickinson Abroad: Organization

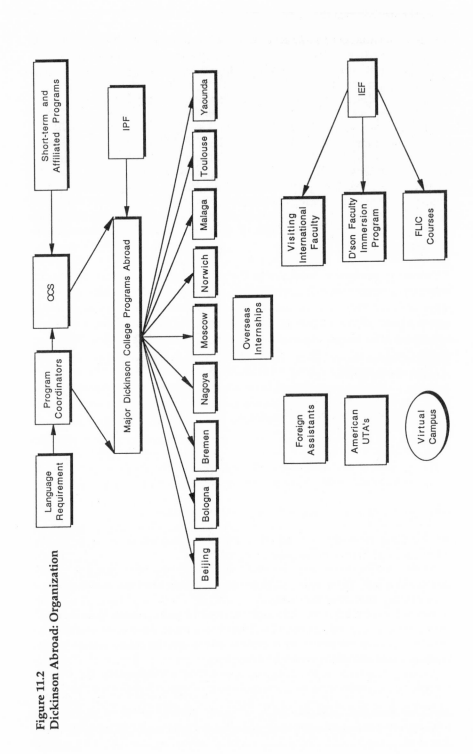

them. Thus, there is no financial reason a student cannot study abroad. As a result, many faculty, particularly in the languages and area study programs, talk in terms of *when* a student will go abroad, rather than *if* he or she will go.

Many of the major areas or programs of study, such as foreign languages, International Studies, International Business and Management, and the Latin American Certificate Program, while not requiring foreign study, are constructed such that a student who is not familiar with a foreign civilization will be disadvantaged in relation to his or her peers who have studied abroad. In some majors almost the entire junior class is abroad, creating the need to maintain and even encourage higher enrollments in post-language-requirement courses. This structure is in part responsible for the vitality of language clubs, housing, and tables, as well as foreign film series, internationally-oriented lectures, and the like, which serve as recruiting tools for programs and as mechanisms for keeping interest high. Coordination of the overseas programs is provided by the Office of Off-Campus Studies, staffed by persons who have had faculty status and long overseas experience, and who speak foreign languages. As a result, over the past five years, 48 percent of the student body has studied abroad for a summer, a semester, or a full academic year, with most leaving for an extended period of time. Two-thirds of these students study in a Dickinson program.

BUDGETARY SELF-SUFFICIENCY

The breadth and relatively rapid growth of the overseas component has created challenges to our infrastructure. An early and highly significant decision was made to separate the budgets of these programs from the general budget of the college. This structure, not commonly found elsewhere, insulates the programs from the competing claims of other campus constituencies that vie for general funds. It also makes the overseas programs fiscally accountable and requires that they stand on their own financially. Consequently, commitment to their success is encouraged by all concerned with them, since insulation from the ups and downs of the general budget also means self-sufficiency and being weaned from it.

Due to this financial independence, a novel steering group, the International Programs Fund Committee (IPF) was formed. This oversight committee, composed of the dean of the college, the treasurer, the director of Off-Campus Studies, and two faculty members who represent the college's Academic Program Committee and Priorities and Budget Committee oversee the financial well-being of the foreign centers. While each program's budget is prepared by the concerned faculty or faculty director and the director of Off-Campus Studies, all-year or summer-immersion programs are required to tithe either a flat fee or a per-head amount to a pool of monies that is administered by the IPF. If a program does not meet its budget in a given year, it is entitled to dip into the IPF pool to make up its shortfall. A program may do this only for three years, after which it faces intense scrutiny and possible cancellation. Any surplus generated by a program reverts to the same pool of money to be recycled to the general good of all programs when required. The fund has been used to buy computers for our overseas centers, buy or lease automobiles for the directors, effect repairs on college-owned overseas property, buy furnishings, or help establish relationships with foreign universities and faculty.

SOURCE OF SCHOLARS

The good relations that so many Dickinson overseas directors have carefully nurtured over the years have netted the home campus a steady stream of foreign visiting faculty. Sixty-one foreign colleagues have visited the campus since 1985, some as Fulbright Scholars, but most as Visiting International Scholars who come from the universities where Dickinson's overseas programs are established. They typically spend from two weeks to two semesters on campus giving lectures, sitting in on seminars, overseeing independent studies, or teaching entire courses. Funded largely by NEH grant monies, these scholars reveal Dickinson's global reach to freshman and sophomore students, while they extend the junior year abroad experience to returning seniors.

As part of the relationship that is established with foreign host universities, the college welcomes ten to 12 foreign assistants annually who work in various departments, particularly in foreign languages. They have created an international table (distinct from the foreign language tables) to promote informal cross-cultural exchange between foreign students and Americans, and they deliver foreign language radio broadcasts on the college radio station assisted by Dickinson students in the foreign languages. Foreign assistants also staff the language tables, foreign language houses and the multicultural house. Moreover, selected senior students who have returned from a full junior year abroad in one of Dickinson's programs can utilize their language proficiency as undergraduate teaching assistants in beginning and intermediate language courses. More than just homework correctors, they are mentored by faculty who work shoulder to shoulder with them in first- and second- year foreign language courses as drill monitors, small discussion group leaders, and coaches.

The permanence of our overseas centers has enabled the college to begin to build internship sites abroad. Much in demand by students, these academic credit-bearing internships take place in private industry and businesses, government agencies, and educational establishments. The overseas directors are responsible for site selection, following students through the internship, and finding qualified readers to evaluate the academic component of the internship. In some areas, local conditions make it difficult to procure full-semester academic internships. In this case, students may accomplish shorter, non-credit field experiences. Dickinson's major in International Business and Management (IB&M), recognizing the value of such experience to students and future employers alike, has mandated an internship or field experience as a major requirement. It is expected that many IB&M majors will complete this requirement abroad.

In retrospect, it is clear that the creation of a broad-spectrum overseas program within a period of ten years was an ambitious and enviable task. All programs of globalization are evolutionary, but the maximum effort required to put a comprehensive program into operation can be exhausting in the short term. The work required left many of the program creators gasping for breath. On a small campus where collegial cooperation rather than outsourcing to a higher level of bureaucracy is essential, the considerable effort required to globalize thoroughly cannot be overstated. Yet, because many are frequently called upon to review, update, and improve the overseas ventures, it is the shared understanding of program creators, overseas directors, and on-campus administrators that the global extension of the campus has become a common cause in which to enlist the freely-given creative talents of many. Thus, Dickinson's overseas infrastructure acts not only as the motor of globalization, but an adhesive that cements faculty and administrative concerns.

MOVING BEYOND THE REQUIRED MINIMUM

As the foregoing discussion suggests, the enhancement of study abroad programs had considerable impact beyond the foreign language departments. As a general matter, the extension of international education out from the core of foreign language majors was a critical imperative in Dickinson's effort to globalize the campus. In part, the college's graduation requirements, which include foreign language and a comparative civilizations course, guarantee some international exposure to the entire student body, as illustrated in Figure 11.1. They make up, in terms of the imagery of concentric circles, the irreducible minimum of the outer group. Yet, real success in international education could come only through the development of a strong middle circle—the movement of a significant cohort of students not intending to become foreign language majors beyond the required minimum.

Dickinson has been able to develop this intermediate group, our version of a vital center, in a variety of ways. For example, the college has a strong tradition of interdisciplinary endeavor, so much so that one-quarter of the most recent graduating class had interdisciplinary majors. These include strong East Asian, Latin American, and Russian Area Study programs and a popular International Studies (IS) major. The latter in particular was restructured over a decade ago in a fashion that makes it a perfect bridge between the foreign language departments and the social sciences. IS majors are required not only to complete a core in international relations (course work in economics, history, and political science), but also to "specialize" in the culture of a single nation through advanced work in language, literature, history, and study abroad. In fact, many students choose to double major in IS and foreign language. This model has been so successful that the college has used it as a template for its new major in International Business and Management. Like IS, IB&M requires both a business/economics core and an area concentration in advanced foreign language and civilization.

VALIDATING THE LANGUAGE REQUIREMENT

A further technique for strengthening both the core and intermediate circles of the international education program has been foreign language across the curriculum. As Dickinson began to transform its campus through globalization, it became apparent that integrating the foreign languages across the campus would be a necessary ingredient in broadening the college's global orientation. It seemed obvious that the integration of foreign language materials in nonforeign language courses would make the particular perspectives of foreign civilizations available to the content of the course in ways not accessible in translation. It was also evident that the opportunity to enhance students' language abilities outside the foreign language classroom, particularly for non-language majors, would not only have intrinsic merit, but validate the college's foreign language requirement as a tool for influencing the totality of college study and research.

As on many college campuses, Dickinson was fortunate to have a number of faculty colleagues in each of its three divisions who had significant foreign language training and proficiency. Others were actively using their graduate school reading knowledge of a foreign language in their research. These colleagues were to become the core of the foreign language-across-the-curriculum project. To refresh their skills and reimmerse them in the culture of the target language, in 1984 Dickinson decided to use part of its NEH grant to offer an unusual series of faculty immersion programs abroad. Each year, the faculty is polled as to the target language they would most like to develop. A group of seven to ten faculty members spends four to five weeks during the following summer in a target language country in which we have a study center. Since 1984, faculty groups have gone to France, Italy, Spain, Germany, and Russia. Before departure, faculty members must have demonstrated intermediate level proficiency in the language. If they have not achieved this level, they take courses in the foreign language on campus. Many take postintermediate level classes. A member of the foreign language department in the target language organizes the summer's work in cooperation with our overseas program and accompanies the group. Many of the participants stay in homes, often those of the colleague at the foreign host university with whom he or she is paired. These pairings ensure that during the stay, scientists talk with other scientists, historians with historians, and the like. In many cases, international friendships have taken root, the opportunity for exchanges of lectures or lengthier stays takes place, and in several cases, collaborative scholarly work with published results has evolved. The participants are also provided with funds from the library for the direct purchase of materials that will relate to the foreign language intensive course (FLIC) they will be teaching upon return.

There are now about 60 colleges and universities in the country that have language-across-the-curriculum programs. Dickinson's program is expressed in a series of about 20 FLIC courses offered throughout the curriculum each semester. We follow an "inclusion" model, whereby materials in the foreign language in which the instructor is competent are included in the course. Assignments vary according to the students' foreign language proficiency. Thus, a beginning student may read three or four paragraphs, while a student who has studied abroad may read whole books or watch original-version films. Those faculty who have high oral proficiency in the language may chat in their offices with students who have similar proficiency. Students may write one-page resumés or whole term papers in the foreign language. We have also seen some informal pairings of faculty in what has been called the "parallel" model, whereby like-minded faculty offer pairs of FLIC courses in parallel subject areas, such as a German course in late nineteenth-century literature and an art history course in German expressionism.

Foreign language intensive courses currently include offerings like "Alternative Economic Systems" (German or Spanish), "Lenin and the Russian Revolution" (Russian), "Security Under Anarchy" (French, German, or Italian), and "Chinese Politics" (Chinese). In our model, faculty interest has always been extraordinarily high, motivated of course by the prospects of spending a summer abroad, but also as a means to create interesting possibilities for student participation and interaction. On the other hand, our students are rewarded for having completed a FLIC course only by mention on their transcript and by the insights they derive from having woven original foreign language materials into the content of a course. They receive no extra course credit. Consequently, the number of students who choose the FLIC option in a course depends entirely on student motivation and, particularly, the persuasive powers of the instructor. Where instructors assume students will complete the foreign language intensive option in their course, and when they are willing to tailor materials for students at varying levels of linguistic proficiency, the FLIC option enrollments are high. For the future, we want to strengthen the program through the appointment of a faculty member who will have released time to coordinate all foreign language offerings, and by the assignment of fluent senior teaching assistants to these courses.

Although Dickinson's forward movement in international education has been exceptionally rapid since the 1980s, much remains to be done. The college has, for instance, begun to develop opportunities for science majors to study abroad. The new International Business & Management program will enroll its first majors in fall 1997. Our experience thus far has, however, led us to a contradictory but important conclusion about transforming a campus through international education.

On the one hand, globalization is a demanding process in terms of personnel, expense, and planning. Programs abroad, for example, place very heavy demands upon the departments expected to staff them. Faculty must be hired and tenured not only on the basis of teaching skill and scholarship, but also their ability to administer. As overseas study expands, college-wide enrollment projections must be altered, and—given the volatility of world affairs—made flexible enough to accommodate significant, unexpected swings prompted by a Chernobyl explosion or terrorist act. Foreign language-across-the-curriculum programs demand considerable investment in faculty development. Effective international and area studies concentrations require a willingness on the part of collaborating departments, such as history and political science, to hire faculty with geography in mind.

On the other hand, institutional payoffs of a comprehensive approach to international education can be very substantial, easily offsetting many of the costs. The establishment of relationships with foreign universities in building overseas programs, for instance, creates a network of contacts for visiting professors and scholars. Residency of a faculty member from a partner university abroad becomes more than an ephemeral event, as the visitor returns home ready to serve as a resource for students going overseas. Pooling the resources of a series of abroad programs helps create economies of scale, and guards individual programs against currency fluctuations, short-term slips in enrollment, and other vicissitudes. Attractive, accessible opportunities for study abroad can significantly reduce student interest in transferring. Offering faculty across the curriculum the opportunity to improve language skills encourages a richer international perspective in disciplinary courses and can lead to new directions in scholarship as well.

Most importantly, a strong, campus-suffusing program in international education prompts students to take this dimension of their educational experience more seriously. They come to see the world beyond our borders not in terms of a foreign language graduation requirement to be completed, or a place to visit for a semester or two. Rather, they integrate the world into their basic understanding of the purposes of undergraduate education and, as a result, of their lives as well.

Chapter 12

A "Globaliberal" Arts Approach: The International Studies Major and the Next Millennium

Nanette S. Levinson

As we approach the next millennium, the challenges of modern global society call for in-depth immersion into a region's culture, as well as a functional specialization and a broad liberal arts foundation. Crafting a successful undergraduate major that meets these challenges is not an easy task. It requires recognition of external trends, both general and those particular to higher education. What are the most important of these trends?

We are no longer a bipolar world. Communications-related technologies are converging, linking the world in ever more complex ways. We are experiencing the globalization of technology, economics, and knowledge. At the same time, regionalization, such as the European Union or the North American Free Trade Agreement; and de-centralization, specifically, a movement away from federalism, are increasing. In the corporate sector, downsizing and career instability are on the upswing. Increasing complexity and uncertainty are leading to leitmotifs of change and connections. These connections serve to decrease uncertainty and match an increasingly complex environment.

Higher education itself is seeing numerous changes, although in the United States there appears to be much less "reengineering" in higher education than in other sectors. The number of liberal arts colleges has declined, while the competition for resources and students has increased. Converging telecommunication and information-related technologies constitute an opportunity and a challenge for college campuses. Finally,

---

"Globaliberal" is a term coined by the author of this chapter to reflect an approach to internationalization that matches trends in the general environment, higher education, and multinational corporations.

there is a focus on student-centered learning and on doing-anchored learning.

AN "OUTCOMES" DEFINITION OF LIBERAL ARTS

While there are many different definitions of liberal arts in higher education, I prefer those definitions that focus on the outcomes of a liberal arts education as opposed to descriptions of what the liberal arts is or is not. Two definitions that fall in the latter category describe the liberal arts as: "the humanities, life sciences, natural sciences, and the social sciences, including psychology" (Gilbert 1995), or state that, "liberal arts educate rather than train; . . . the absence of undergraduate professional education" (Breneman 1994). An example of the former comes from Marden and Engerman. They write that the liberal arts achieve "the undermining of parochialism, an openness to new ideas, the acquisition of effective communication skills, and an ability to see ideas in their full complexity; a cross-disciplinary goal of intellectual and personal development" (Marden and Engerman 1992).

In examining these definitions, I agree with those who argue that an international agenda complements a liberal arts orientation. An international agenda builds on the liberal arts and offers study abroad opportunities as well as study of a foreign language. But as we approach the new millennium, colleges and universities need to go beyond an international agenda to offer what I call a globaliberal approach. Such an approach best matches those trends outlined earlier, both in the general environment and in higher education. It parallels developments in the international business sector where multinational corporations once opened up offices in other parts of the world but directed decision making and operations from a core, often U.S.-based headquarters. Today's multinational corporations are rapidly exhibiting a more global orientation, including global marketing efforts; multiple, cross-national communication paths; and myriad alliance memberships, most of which are not geographically tethered.

Similar to liberal arts, the term globalization has multiple meanings. The most commonly used definitions center around globalization's references to crossing or even transcending national boundaries, and to increasing inter-connections and complexities. Thus, I define a globaliberal approach as one that achieves an ability to see, understand, and deal with interconnections as well as with complexity, and uses a cross-disciplinary stance effectively to manage the multidimensional, including cultures, complexities, connections, and change. When we talk about international, we most often mean cross-national and often two countries; but when I use the term global, I include the nation-state (even two nations-states!) and go beyond, to capture the complexity of interconnections within and across borders, as well as the concomitant strategic reorientations. Thus, a globaliberal model must also go beyond the provision of study abroad and foreign language acquisition to educate students and faculty to comprehend domestic/international, political/economic, and multiple-level, cultural cross-connections.

A GLOBALIBERAL MODEL

American University's School of International Service, the largest school of international affairs in the United States with over 2,000 students and 54 full-time faculty, has designed a learning experience for undergraduates that can indeed be called a globaliberal experience. The model consists of three closely interrelated parts: a strong liberal arts core, globaliberal studies, and cocurricular components.

The core consists of two courses each in the following areas: college writing, creative arts, traditions that shape the Western world, social institutions and behavior, natural sciences, and non-Western area studies. This core strengthens cross-disciplinary, critical thinking, and key communication abilities. Students have course choices within each of these areas, including choices of two course sequences that achieve depth as well as breadth. Building on this core, the model requires a strong foundation in world politics, economics, research methods, and statistics, as well as foreign language study. It also includes international foundation courses in four components: international communication/cross-cultural communication, international development, international economics, and foreign policy—the four pillars of understanding globalization complexities today and in the new millennium.

The globaliberal curricular model includes requirements for two multidisciplinary specializations, a regional concentration from one of six areas of the world selected by the student and a functional concentration. The regional concentration involves a humanities- and a social science-based immersion into that region. Students learn about the history, culture, literature, politics, and economies of their particular region. The region also matches the student's foreign language focus. The functional concentration involves a multidisciplinary foray into one of the following: international and cross-cultural communication, international development, international economic policy, Islamic studies, international peace and conflict resolution, international politics, international law and organization, or foreign policy. Concentration studies ensure an understanding of the connection between domestic and international, and cross-national and global. (See Figure 12.1 for the foundation, concentration, and capstone elements.)

The capstone experiences build on the regional and functional concentrations. They allow students to integrate, apply, and actively learn as an appropriate conclusion to the four-year model. Choosing a study abroad or exchange experience (ranging from a traditional semester or two

Figure 12.1
A Globaliberal Model: The School of International Service Experience

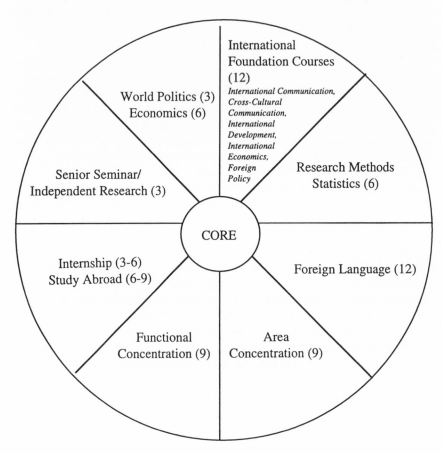

semesters abroad, to summer or spring break experiences) and/or doing an international internship anywhere in the world provide one element of the capstone experience. The other element is a Senior Seminar which allows students to conduct independent, in-depth research, complementing and integrating their core studies, as well as their area and functional concentrations. The Senior Seminar experience also includes an oral presentation of independent research and an overall assessment of the undergraduate experience rooted in the globaliberal approach.

This model, however, would be incomplete without its cocurricular components, which begin with unique experiences in the freshman year, even before students actually attend a class. Prior to freshman orientation, students enroll in the Freshman International Experience, a four- to five-day small group immersion into international and intercultural issues, literatures, and ways of thinking. During the day, each small group, led by a peer mentor from the sophomore or junior class, engages in volunteer work related to the international experience. For example, one group might do an action research project to assist a refugee rights group, or another might do volunteer work with a resettlement organization. In the evenings, students meet with faculty and policy leaders in Washington, D.C. in an informal setting to discuss the issues they are encountering. These interactions, set in an idea-sharing environment, link students to one another, to faculty and other experts, and to their upcoming curricular experiences. Whether it's a discussion centered around a novel related to the volunteer experience or a film such as *El Norte*, students are introduced to active learning, and forge informal linkages among themselves, with upperclassmen and faculty even before the first class starts.

Additionally, during the freshman year, students participate in a spring miniexternship program, during which students are linked to an alumnus or alumna of the international affairs program. The externship experience provides both role models and an opportunity to experience one set of connections between theory and practice.

Moving to the sophomore and junior years, students have opportunities for peer advising and leadership development, which allow them to demonstrate an understanding of the elements of a globaliberal arts major and its benefits. They also have opportunities for leadership in student government, at the school and university levels, and in activities such as Model UN programs, both on campus and in the community.

Throughout their four years, students also participate in a contemporary international issues series, offered monthly. This series brings together students, faculty, and external experts on topics of timely public interest and public dialogue. Finally, to complement the formal Senior Seminar that serves as a capstone experience for this model, students also participate in a noncredit Senior Seminar Series during their final year on campus. Planned jointly with students, this series, "Global 2006: Key Issues for a Transitional Decade," brings leaders to campus in a range of fields from public, private, and not-for-profit sectors. Each leader describes the challenges he or she sees in the decade ahead, connecting what students have learned, their skills of critical inquiry, their own research efforts, and the issues they will face during the decade following graduation. Examples of leaders participating in the 1996 version of the Senior Seminar Series include: the Honorable Alan Simpson from the U.S. Senate, and the Honorable Michael Armacost, President of the Brookings Institution and the former U.S. Ambassador to Japan. Overall, the cocurricular components are critical in providing students opportunities for active learning and bridging theory and practice.

CRITICAL SUCCESS FACTORS

Key to the success of this model is faculty involvement, not only in the design of each curricular element, but also in a collegial effort to look at the interconnections among model elements, and especially between the co-curricular and curricular elements. Individual faculty sponsor and supervise international internships; they are active as mentors, especially with regard to study abroad experiences. Indeed, faculty serve as champions for quality and interactive learning and for developing those skills so critical for coping with globalization. The faculty also provide opportunities for students to be involved in their own research projects—projects that often are at the cutting edge of international studies.

As is evident from the diagram highlighting our globaliberal arts model, there is both structure and flexibility inherent in such a model. But this requires advising—another critical success factor. The School of International Service uses professional advisors (a staff of three, with one specifically devoted to freshmen advising) to ensure the quality of the undergraduate learning experience. Professional advisors complement individual faculty advising with regard to research interests, study abroad opportunities, and the like.

Another factor critical to success is cocurricular anchoring and echoing. The total undergraduate experience should be a seamless one for students; the boundaries between cocurricular and curricular should echo the seamless connections forged by increasing globalization in the world at large. Cocurricular activities need to reinforce curricular objectives and vice versa. This echoing and anchoring, a complex combination, allows students to see and demonstrate the connection between ideas and actions—a connection so vital to an understanding of the upcoming millennium.

Finally, the presence of alliances, the involvement of the individual student, as well as the overall program in a series of network connections, contribute significantly to the success of the learning experience. Such alliances include exchange programs that place U.S. students and faculty with other universities around the world, informal and formal connections with transnational organizations, membership in consortia that cross national boundaries, and exchange programs that bring students and faculty from other parts of the world to this campus. These are just a few of the alliance opportunities that serve as critical success factors; the opportunity to participate in such alliances ensures the success of the globaliberal arts model's implementation. To be an educated citizen of the next millennium requires not only an understanding of globalization, but a linkage between ideas and action—between being a participant in a series of cross-cutting and cross-national networks and being able to generate, critique, and disseminate ideas in such a context.

I began by talking about a key trend in our changing world: the globalization of technology, economics, and knowledge. What I have conveyed is a model which evidences the initial globalization of higher education. The process of curricular construction and learning experience design is, indeed, an iterative one. Universities are truly learning organizations (Levinson and Asahi 1995). New ideas for undergraduate experiences, such as the globaliberal arts approach at American University's School of International Service, are proliferating. As globalization and regionalization ensue, universities, much like governments and industries, are changing their orientations and practices. We are on the verge of a new era that is information-based and connections-centered. The globaliberal arts approach presented here is a beginning. The next iteration may even more vividly reflect globalization and regionalization forces.

REFERENCES

Breneman, D. W. 1994. *Liberal Arts Colleges: Thriving, Surviving, or Endangered?* Washington, D.C.: Brookings Institution.

Gilbert, J. 1995. "The Liberal Arts College—Is It Really an Endangered Species?" *Change* 27, no. 5: 37-43.

Levinson, Nanette and Minoru Asahi. 1995. "Cross-national Alliances and Interorganizational Learning." *Organizational Dynamics* 24, no. 2 (autumn): 50-63.

Marden, Parker G. and David C. Engerman. 1992. "In the International Interest: Liberal Arts Colleges Take the High Road." *Educational Record* 73, no. 2 (spring): 42-46.

Chapter 13

International Studies as a Growth Strategy for a Small Liberal Arts College

James J. Ward and Jane Tyler Ward

Cedar Crest College, 129 years old in 1996, is a private, four-year liberal arts college for women in southeastern Pennsylvania. With a strong academic reputation, but only modestly endowed and drawing most of its students from a regional pool, Cedar Crest is typical of the so-called "second tier" of women's colleges. Thus it experienced the demographic and economic difficulties of the 1970s and 1980s in much the same measure as many of its sister institutions. Faced with declining enrollments and consequent financial stress, the college resorted to various programmatic and tactical adjustments; for example, introducing new employment or career-oriented majors and aggressively marketing its continuing education program. At best, these responses purchased short-term relief from the larger, structural pressures. They also brought serious negative effects, most notably a blurring of the college's identity and a deepening distrust between faculty and the upper administration. At the same time, enrollment-weakened programs were starved of resources, faculty salaries declined vis-à-vis comparable institutions, and the college's once gracious physical facilities fell into disrepair. In short, all the makings of genuine crisis were at hand.

In 1987, the trustees of Cedar Crest and Muhlenberg, a neighboring coeducational college with which several joint programs already existed, began negotiations toward a possible merger, or as it was euphemized, "affiliation." The story of these deliberations is a tale in its own right, but need not be reprised here. It soon became evident that far more separated the two colleges than prospectively joined them, and the initiative was abandoned on both sides. In retrospect, the failure of the merger project provided Cedar Crest with a defining moment. Coincident with the appointment of a new president, the trustees authorized an ambitious program for the revitalization of the college—a departure from their previous fiduciary approach characterized by frugality and conservatism. Putting to rest questions of affiliation and coeducation, the college reaffirmed its identity as a women's institution, and both trustees and the alumnae association—the latter energized by the fight over affiliation— guaranteed substantial new resources. With the inauguration of President Dorothy Gulbenkian Blaney in 1989, and supported by $5 million in new funding, the college invested in the rehabilitation of its campus, significant salary improvement, increased financial aid to students, and a recruitment program to reverse the enrollment declines of the previous decade.

Quickly put, the last six or seven years have seen a genuine renaissance at Cedar Crest. Enrollment is at an all-time high, spurred by an overall increase of more than 80 percent since 1990. Annual giving has more than doubled, and alumnae support is higher than ever. We have successfully marketed an $11 million bond issue and have secured pledges for just under half of the total needed in the prepublic phase of a $12.5 million capital campaign. Ground was recently broken for a new multipurpose science and arts center, and the college will initiate its first master's program in 1996-97. These new levels of credibility and accomplishment have earned consistent *U.S. News and World Report* top-tier rankings for Northeastern liberal arts colleges.

BUILDING FROM WITHIN

On the academic side of its renewal, Cedar Crest resolved, quite pragmatically, to concentrate on building excellence in areas where it was already strong and well-reputed—the creative and performing arts; the sciences, particularly in connection with environment and health care; and innovative teaching and learning, specifically as these apply to women. In addition, the college committed itself to internationalizing its curriculum and campus life. This was signaled by the appearance of an under-secretary general of the United Nations as the principal speaker for President Blaney's inauguration, and furthered through a series of high-visibility lecture visits to the college by ambassadors and other international representatives from Washington and New York. Anecdotally, it was through this matrix of associations that a group of students and faculty secured an invited visit to the Iraqi Mission in New York at the height of the Kuwaiti crisis in the winter of 1990-91.

To rehearse here the rationale for internationalizing Cedar Crest's educational program would be redundant. Of more interest are the key strategic decisions made, and the process by which internationalization has been promoted in the curriculum. Certain approaches were excluded by the college's circumstances after two decades of struggle, confusion, and conflict. Other priorities had more urgent claim on the new financial resources being accumulated—the deteriorated campus, for example. A search for major external funding was premature, until the college could demonstrate the success of its strategic turnaround. Existing programs with proven student appeal and identified as areas of excellence had to be sustained. New faculty were unlikely to be added, and new capabilities, such as technology or library services, would have to come in conjunction with or through contribution by existing programs. Basically, internationalization had to be accomplished with materials at hand, and the curricular centerpiece—an international studies program—built from within.

The college's internal political landscape also dictated certain constraints. Though small in total number, the faculty was divided among several strong and largely autonomous departments. Through all the stresses of the preceding years, most departments had managed to preserve themselves, and all exercised vigilance over the general curriculum as well as their individual programs. While three or four new departments had been created since the 1970s, a more congenial model was the addition of new programs—e.g., certificate programs—within existing departments. For the size of its faculty and its enrollment, the college had enough majors. Little political support for the addition of a new, freestanding major program in international studies could be assumed.

Preparing a proposal for internationalizing the curriculum was assigned to a study group, of which Professor James Ward of the History and Political Science Department was chair. This group met numerous times in the summer and fall of 1993. It had use of the proceedings of two prior working groups on internationalization. It also reviewed a number of existing programs at other colleges, as well as the ample professional literature on the subject. The study group included representatives of the departments likely to contribute courses to the projected international studies major, and the group solicited participation by other faculty who, by their teaching and research areas, would be interested in the proposal to be developed. In essence, we were practicing politics aimed at increasing support and disarming potential opposition.

Not surprisingly, the study group's recommendations, presented in October 1993, called for continuing and strengthening several ongoing activities that contributed an international dimension to the college. Among these were enhanced study abroad opportunities, increased enrollment of foreign students, support for campus chapters of such organizations as Amnesty International and Greenpeace, and continuation of the program of public affairs lectures by UN and U.S. ambassadors. In regard to curriculum, the study group encouraged departments to incorporate greater international content into existing courses and develop new courses specifically addressed to global topics. Curricular instruments already in place, such as interdisciplinary freshman and junior seminars and the college-wide honors program, were also recommended for greater attention to international subjects. The study group endorsed the college's initiatives to bring new educational technologies to the campus, most notably computerizing classrooms and dormitories, and providing faculty and students with electronic mail and Internet access.

The academic centerpiece for internationalization—an international studies program—had to be advanced with greater finesse. The faculty was unlikely to approve another new, independent major; that is, sanction a new department, if for no other reasons than concern over staffing and possible draw-offs from existing resource allocation. Nor was the faculty inclined to approve an extensive list of new international studies courses, for the same reasons. Instead, the study group proposed an International Studies (IS) Co-Major Program, which students could take only in conjunction with another major in an existing department. The precedent for this format existed with the education co-major and some of the professional certificate programs, which require concurrent completion of a discipline-based major.

THE CO-MAJOR APPROACH

The IS co-major is constructed as a sequence of courses, frequently allowing the student a choice of options, primarily in history, political science, economics, sociology and anthropology, and communication studies. A foreign language requirement—at least two courses at the intermediate or advanced level—is included. Only two new courses were proposed, an entry-level course, "Introduction to International Studies," and a "Senior Seminar in International Studies." To progress through the program, the student begins with two introductory courses, the "Introduction to International Studies" and an existing course in the history department, "Origins of the Contemporary World," and proceeds through a sequence of intermediate and advanced courses, concluding with the Senior Seminar. The total credit requirement for the IS major is 36 or 42, counting the six-credit foreign language requirement. This puts the IS co-major within the common range of credit requirements for most Cedar Crest majors, between 30 and 42 credits, or one-quarter to one-third of the student's total credits to graduate.

Some details of the new program are important to note. Because it is a co-major, international studies had to be articulated with majors in other fields, specifically the disciplines that contribute most strongly to the new program: history, politics, economics, sociology, and communications. To demonstrate this articulation, the study group developed several models showing how students could fulfill their major and co-major requirements within a reasonable credit load. As an example, with several courses counting toward both majors, students can complete the history and international studies combination with 57 credits, which is less than half the total credit requirement for graduation. The combination of political science and international studies is similar. Students are therefore left half or more of their undergraduate preparation for general education requirements (many of which are also satisfied in the double major sequence), electives, and internships. These articulations were pragmatically selected to allay faculty concerns about another major taking over substantial parts of the curriculum and to offer students attractive, but manageable, educational combinations.

Because each student chooses her combination of majors and makes a number of selections in the international studies program, a premium is placed on flexibility, as opposed to prescription. Through substitutions and equivalences, students are able to take appropriate special-topic courses when offered, take courses on other campuses, and spend a semester or year studying abroad. It is altogether possible that no two students will follow precisely the same trajectory through the IS Program. Obviously, high importance is attached to responsible course selection by students, and to close and careful consultation with faculty advisors.

The International Studies Co-Major Program was approved by the faculty in the spring of 1994 and came into the curriculum for the 1994-95 academic year. In the two years since, it has attracted a small, but interesting number of students who have put together combinations of international studies with psychology and philosophy, which were not initially anticipated. The more probable combinations, with history and political science, are also represented. These are but modest accomplishments, commensurate perhaps with the actual resources committed to the program. Still, interest in the IS co-major is regularly expressed at admissions preview events and among transfer students who have had some previous work in similar programs. The linkage with study abroad and overseas internships and the possibility for employment with some international dimension should enhance the IS co-major's appeal.

CRITICAL REVIEW

Two years' experience with the International Studies Co-Major Program allows some tentative assessments. International studies is primarily identified with history and political science, the department where it is administratively housed. At a college with a tradition of strong departments, a program without a department of its own ends up an orphan, or at best, a stepchild. This should not altogether be attributed to imperialism by the historians and political scientists. Faculty changes in other contributing departments have removed some teaching competencies, and more importantly, personal commitments to the IS co-major. To state the obvious, without personal advocacy and visibility in the classroom, the tie between catalog program and individual professor quickly erodes. The last thing desired, however, is that international studies be perceived as merely an adjunct to history and political science; this is a disservice to the former and an additional burden on the latter, which already have enough associated programs.

It was hoped that faculty who contribute courses to the IS Program would manifest a certain coherence and solidarity. The initial proposal recommended regular consultation among these faculty, exchanging syllabi and co-advising students. Occasional, small-scale workshops were suggested to bring together faculty and students in the IS Program. These ideas have only partially materialized, largely due to the all-too-many other responsibilities and demands ordinarily confronting faculty in small liberal arts colleges. The new introductory course in international studies was offered once or twice in an interdisciplinary team-taught format; but again, because of faculty shifts, this has now become a single faculty assignment, although it moves among different disciplines. Despite a generous program of faculty development grants, faculty have chosen not to participate in, for example, the international seminars offered by the Council on International Educational Exchange or similar organizations. Rather, the pull of discipline-based research and pedagogical upgrades in one's own field have asserted priority. While the college did fund group faculty development trips to Russia and Central Europe in 1994 and 1995, these have had only tangential impact on the IS Program.

Cedar Crest belongs to a consortium with four other liberal arts colleges and Lehigh University, the Lehigh Valley Association of Independent Colleges. Yet, consortium arrangements for study abroad and other international initiatives had not been realized in the measure projected a few years ago. The explanations for this are too cumbersome to entertain here. However, a regular exchange of faculty among the several campuses does provide students the opportunity to take additional courses with international reach or content. One final point: In 1996, we adopted new general education requirements—essentially a more structured and objective-defined central curriculum—which no doubt will have some consequence for the content and sequencing of courses that serve the international studies co-major. Most immediately, we have dropped the general requirement for foreign language proficiency, allowing instead individual departments to establish language requirements of their own (which for many will be none at all). The language requirement in the IS co-major, which will be continued, may therefore become a disadvantage in attracting students otherwise interested, but disinclined to learn a second tongue.

INTERNATIONAL STUDENTS REINVIGORATE CAMPUS

The initiative for internationalizing the student body began in 1989 with the arrival of President Dorothy Gulbenkian Blaney. Dr. Blaney came from an international background, having lived and worked in Europe, as well as having strong ties to the international community in New York City. In 1989, Cedar Crest students came from a relatively homogeneous background, largely selected from eastern Pennsylvania, New Jersey, and New York. Although we had drawn students from international backgrounds, we had not instituted an international recruiting effort and, as a result, did not have a critical mass of international students. President Blaney immediately strengthened recruitment of international students. Since that time, we have grown to 44 international students from 18 different countries. We also have ongoing two- to three-week language and culture programs with colleges and universities in Japan, Germany, Sweden, and Denmark. The director of international programs manages a strong English as a Second Language (ESL) Program, as well as working with the Cosmopolitan Club, one of the most active and prestigious clubs on campus, and other international directors in our local consortium. Although the first few years were difficult, international students have brought a new vitality and permanently changed the milieu of the college.

Essentially, growth and development of the program progressed through three stages. The first stage could be called "clueless." Representatives from the college visited Japan, Puerto Rico, Taiwan, and Hong Kong. Applications were encouraged from Africa, the Middle East, and the Indian subcontinent. An international admissions recruiter was hired to develop ties with agencies abroad. The dean of students was often the person to meet international students at the bus station or airport. We had no formal ESL Program, and did not know how to place students in classes to make the transition easier for those with limited English skills. We were not knowledgeable with regard to the impact of cultural differences on roommate issues, our very Western honor code, or the necessity for international students to have a place to live year-round. Japanese agencies in particular sent us students who would stay for a year and move on to the "big city." However, with a tremendous amount of goodwill and a true commitment to internationalization, we learned from our experiences, decided to put more money into the program, and made the necessary changes.

The college entered the second stage, an "intercultural interlude," with a new director of intercultural students, programs developed for cultural awareness in the residence halls, training of faculty, placement of students in courses they could handle, and an ESL Program. As our experiences broadened, we began to seriously address cultural differences, prejudice, and language problems. For example, when the local Ku Klux Klan left calling cards in one of the residence halls housing Japanese students, we asked one of our history professors, an expert on the Klan, to lead discussions with small groups of residence hall directors, international "buddies," and faculty. Proactively, we assigned every international student an international buddy, who was trained to answer questions, help with transportation, and generally be a friend. We held prejudice reduction workshops for faculty and students, trained staff, and added ESL classes. We changed the focus of a standing committee, the Cultural Programs

Committee, from classical music and dance programs to one that would incorporate diverse cultural experiences. The committee developed a series of programs every semester based on international and multicultural themes. One year we celebrated a different culture each month in arts and activities programs, food, and lectures. We developed a Freshman Seminar for honors students which focuses on diversity and multicultural issues. The population of international students and indigenous students from diverse cultures was growing—an exciting and challenging time. However, the intercultural director was overburdened with too many responsibilities; from mentor and advisor, to ESL instructor, to director and recruiter for the special programs. This led to a third stage, the "proactive, networking" stage.

We hired a director of international programs and instructor for the ESL Program. The campus began to look more diverse, not as an imposed issue, but a positive outcome of a more broadly interactive campus community. The look of the college changed as the international studies co-major was developed and implemented. Our fall 1995 All Campus Day on internationalism highlighted the Cosmopolitan Club's activities (e.g., dances, food, poetry from other cultures). The director was able to spend more time developing and fine-tuning special orientation programs, since she was not teaching ESL as well. We hired a new director in our Academic Resource Center who was familiar with English literacy and writing issues, and was able to improve the level of help given to individual students. The provost spent two years in Japan teaching ESL at Tezukayama College in Nara, and was thus sensitive to and knowledgeable about academic and communication problems faced by international students.

Cedar Crest anticipates further growth in the international student population. Resident students request international students as roommates. International students have taken leadership positions in residence halls, on the Student Government Association, as instructional assistants for courses, and in their majors. We have encouraged study abroad programs for our students, and see an increasing interest in international programs and the International Studies Co-Major Program. Problems now tend to be of a different nature than those first encountered in 1989 through 1992. For example, one of the major international issues at the moment has to do with reentry into the country of origin, especially for Japanese students. Most students at Cedar Crest include internships in their majors. When Japanese students return to Japan, they are often faced with less-than-professional positions. Also, after the freedom and personal responsibility of living and studying in the United States, it is sometimes difficult for them to return to a more restricted female role. African and Indian graduates have encountered similar problems. The college has now hired a new director of international programs with experience in reentry issues.

New initiatives need to be developed centering not just on countries that can send students who can afford to study abroad, but actively and strategically recruiting students from underrepresented countries. Although the college has generously funded students from South Africa, China, Poland, Russia, and Croatia, a comprehensive strategy for recruiting remains to be determined. In the life of the campus, not only in the academic program, our most important lesson learned is that internationalization is never something that has been completed, but is always in process.

Chapter 14

Mainstreaming International Studies in a Community College

David C. Prejsnar and Alison Tasch

Some of the crucial moral and spiritual challenges of our age are human rights for all peoples, solutions to the ecological crisis brought on by modernization and urbanization, and the need for a sense of community with other cultures and ethnic groups. How can we, as international studies educators, and our students, in the context of the liberal arts curriculum, address these challenges? In particular, how can we address these issues in the face of the increasing importance for our students of career and professional concerns?

These questions should be addressed throughout American higher education and the field of international studies. Postsecondary education in America should include the study of other nations and cultures. As Joseph S. Johnston, Jr. has stated in a recent report by the Association of American Colleges, "To be educated is to have a general knowledge of the larger world, some understanding of the array of individual cultures that constitute it, their interdependence, and the place of one's own culture among them. . . . International education helps undermine received opinions of all types. It can be unsettling and challenging. At its best, however, it fosters personal growth through reflection on one's assumptions, values, and moral choices. It challenges students to confront the relativity of things, but also to make their own grounded judgments (Johnston 1993, 6)." Since about 60 percent of college students currently attend community or two-year colleges, it is vital that international studies in the liberal arts curriculum reach these students, if most Americans are to be considered truly educated in the next century.

The Community College of Philadelphia (CCP) and its faculty have made a commitment to international studies by institutionalizing a new liberal arts curriculum with a requirement for courses with a global perspective and an option in international studies. Through a new Title VI Grant, we have also strengthened course offerings in area studies and become a resource center for Asian studies. We believe our approach represents a replicable model for "mainstreaming" international studies in the community college environment.

PROFILE OF A COMMUNITY COLLEGE

There is a Chinese proverb which might help set the context for our treatment of international studies at the community college level: "A husband and wife share the same bed, but dream different dreams." It could be said that two- and four-year colleges have many of the same dreams for promoting international education, but as they lie in different beds, have to nurture their dreams with very different student demographics and financial circumstances. A national survey recently released by the American Association of Community Colleges indicates that international education is on the agenda of the majority of two-year colleges (Chase and Mahoney 1996). Over 80 percent of the colleges that responded to the survey offered some type of international studies program. A high percentage of the colleges have foreign or immigrant students (80 percent), offer foreign language curricula (64 percent), and have staff or faculty who are responsible for administering an international studies program (61 percent). Perhaps most significantly, approximately 70 percent of the colleges surveyed believed that their international studies program would continue to grow in the near future (1996, 7). These figures indicate that community colleges have made increasing global awareness a major priority for the coming century.

In line with these national trends, Community College of Philadelphia is in the beginning stages of building a substantial international emphasis on the liberal arts. On the other hand, a profile of the college indicates that it is in many respects different from other institutions represented here. Our community college is an urban, non-residential, and open-admissions two-year college. We have a very diverse student body, with the largest group, African Americans, comprising about 47 percent, and Caucasians making up a slightly smaller percentage. Asians and Latinos together are about 11.5 percent of the student population. Many students are academically underprepared, many are poor, and their ages range from about 15 to 95, with an average age of about 26. Almost two-thirds are women. Most students at the college attend part-time. Of the 19,000 students in degree programs (out of about 44,000 students served in some way annually), about 2,000 are immigrants, with many of them refugees and some having had no previous formal study of English. As these figures indicate, almost all of our students are "nontraditional" in some respects, with gaps in their educational backgrounds, as well as wonderfully varied life and cultural experiences. Despite this nontraditional student body,

CCP has had one of the highest rates in the nation of successful transfer to four-year colleges and universities, including the University of Pennsylvania, Bucknell University, Haverford College, and other selective institutions. We have also been included in a Ford Foundation research project on the "culture of success" in community colleges.

Such success cannot be ascribed, however, to lavish resources. We have under $4,500 per year available to spend on the total education of a full-time student, of which over one-third comes from tuition. The state and city governments, with tight budgets and the usual reluctance to raise taxes, have provided no expectation that our funding will catch up with costs any time soon. To keep costs down, the college has been using a large number of adjunct, instead of full-time, faculty.

These limits on our resources have been both a challenge and an opportunity for international education and have helped shape the direction of this growth. For example, we have focused more on curriculum and faculty development than on potentially more expensive student study abroad or faculty exchange, although we are now beginning to develop initiatives in these areas. Similarly, in the late 1970s the college made a decision not to sponsor foreign student visas, perhaps believing that our energies would best be devoted to serving the needs of a large immigrant student population. This decision is now being rethought, and in the near future the college may once again admit international students on an F-1 visa. Even at present, however, the current demographic mixture of nationalities among both students and faculty represents an important resource for increasing global awareness on campus. One example of this is the annual week-long International Festival, which features students and faculty demonstrating customs from around the globe.

INTERNATIONAL STUDIES AS BOTH
REQUIREMENT AND ELECTIVE

Within these economic and political realities, CCP has made a significant commitment in the last five years to international education and has undertaken a number of important initiatives in this area. While much of this work is ongoing, and such a retrospective analysis may imply greater cohesion than is warranted, it is possible to give an account of the steps underway to incorporate global studies into the liberal arts curriculum by focusing on five principles that are helping to guide this process. These principles are:

- development of an international studies curriculum and integration of international education in a curricular context,
- use of existing resources that previously had not been fully directed towards international studies,
- where possible, use of grants to start an initiative and build institutional support for a program,

- institutionalization of the grant-funded initiatives, and
- movement from a mostly "infusion approach" in international studies to a balance between this and an area studies approach.

First, the college has developed a curricular framework in the liberal arts which includes international studies as a general education requirement and an elective course of study. The college also continues to emphasize that all aspects of international education be clearly embedded in a curricular context. We owe students in the liberal arts an excellent global education. Therefore, the college has recently designed and put in place a new liberal arts curriculum, and has made an explicit commitment to including study of international topics at two levels in the curriculum. First, the curriculum requires all students to take a minimum of one social science and one humanities course in international studies. So as not to delay the start of the curriculum, we have largely used existing courses to satisfy this requirement. Courses fulfilling this at present include a reasonable balance of social science and humanities courses, plus more limited possibilities in business. There are courses in the disciplines of geography, environmental studies, world history, interdisciplinary humanities, economics, anthropology, comparative literature, art history, music history, and foreign languages, including French, Spanish, Italian, German, and Arabic. We have thus tried to use our existing resources, where possible.

Secondly, the curriculum offers several options, or tracks, for concentrated study in a particular area or discipline, one of which is international studies. This option requires students to take certain introductory courses in international studies, beyond the general curricular requirement. Students must take two geography courses (either physical or cultural, plus regional geography), and at least one world history course. They are also expected to complete at least one year of foreign language at the intermediate level or above.

Each option in the liberal arts curriculum requires a student to design, in consultation with his or her advisor, a Course Concentration Cluster or "mini-major" of three related courses. Within the International Studies Option, this course concentration must have a well-articulated international focus.

A SAMPLE MINI-MAJOR IN INTERNATIONAL STUDIES

A student in our curriculum who has chosen a concentration of three courses in the International Studies Option might pursue the following combination of courses. The unifying focus of this sample concentration, chosen in consultation with the student's advisor, is "Global Diversity Across Cultures: The Challenges of Cultural Traditions and Modernity." "Modernity," Fredric Jameson argues, "is a concept which is in many ways impossible to understand when we are immersed in it and assume it as our ground, like a fish in water" (Jameson 1993, 7). It is only when we juxtapose the modern with premodern cultural traditions that self-reflective awareness becomes possible. The courses and texts in this course concentration are designed to explore these issues of what it means to be modern, and what we should retain that is valuable from the past as we adapt to new challenges. The student might choose in this concentration to take "Humanities 102: Cultural Traditions," a course that examines Western and other traditions in the humanities from the 1600s to the present. In this course, the student is assigned T. S. Eliot's "The Waste Land," and might also take "Women in Literature," in which he or she is assigned Mariama Bâ's novel, *So Long a Letter*. Finally, the student might choose a new course, "Tradition and Transformation in Japanese History," which studies Japanese cultural history from the early Japanese myths of the Kojiki to the rapid changes after World War II. In this course, the student is asked to read Natsume Soseki's novel of the early twentieth century, *Kokoro*.

Students in the International Studies Option are free to work out individualized course concentrations with their advisors. A concentration similar to the one outlined here has, in fact, been running at the college for the past two years in the Transfer Opportunities Program (TOP). Students in the humanities section of the program take exactly such a three-course concentration focusing on Western, African, and Japanese history and culture. In addition, students take a research paper course (English 102), choosing a topic within one of the three cultural areas. Finally, the 20 to 30 students in the program each semester engage in weekly seminars with the four participating faculty members and participate in trips to area art exhibits, cultural sites, and movies relevant to the Western, African, or Japanese material being studied in the classes.

While these texts would be read as whole works in the courses, for this example, short passages are included to illustrate how deeply the readings delve into the subject. Questions the students would be asked to consider might include: What does this text say or suggest about the relation between cultural traditions and modernity? How do these texts challenge us to rethink the values of our modern society?

We expect our students to read primary texts from diverse cultures and engage in exploration and analytic discussion and writing. We ask them to make connections as they read new material and approach the understanding of cultures both "from the inside out," and in the context of the historical milieu and intertextual references which frame it. These particular texts were chosen in part because they engage related issues, but also because each has particular value for an international studies student.

Eliot's "The Waste Land" (T. S. Eliot 1995, 1,620) is almost unavoidable as a reference point in Western culture, of course. "The Game of Chess" section as an excerpt presents a clear juxtaposition of the voices of older and newer cultural values and idioms. Written in 1922, in a Western cultural context profoundly shaken by World War I, the text juxtaposes voices from ancient to contemporary, and as diverse as Buddhist and Hindu to Cockney music hall. The shades of Shakespeare's Cleopatra, Ariel, and Ophelia haunt a contemporary London where the modern housewife, Lil, has bad teeth and premature aging from a failed abortion, while her husband just "wants a good time."

Anxiety recurs: "Do you know nothing? Do you see nothing? Do you remember nothing?" And the bartender's repeated "Hurry up please it's time" ushers everyone out into the dark. There is a sense of cacophony, of a mostly sordid or neurotic present in which the allusions to the more powerfully shaped meanings of past traditions require footnotes. Still, there are flashes of beauty, energy, a need for a quest among the rubble. "These fragments I have shored against my ruins," says a narrative voice towards the end of the poem. Western modernism, in which "The Waste Land" is a prominent text, values irony, ambiguity, a sense of being deracinated and having to redefine terms, despite the awareness that such new definitions might not accomplish anything.

Natsume Soseki's novel, *Kokoro*, was written in 1914, two years after the death of the Emperor Meiji (Soseki 1957, 242). During the reign of the Meiji Emperor (1868-1912), Japan was transformed from a feudal society to a modern nation-state, able to defeat in war a major European nation (Russia). Soseki is revered by many Japanese as their greatest modern novelist, and *Kokoro* is considered, by both Japanese and Western scholars, a definitive work which captures the tensions and ambiguities felt at the end of the Meiji era. The term *kokoro* in Japanese can mean both heart and mind; the novel can be read as Soseki's examination of "the heart of things," that which lies at the heart of the modern. It tells the story of a teacher-student relationship between an unnamed narrator, a university student, and Sensei (teacher). The excerpt, from towards the end of the novel, shows the character Sensei as he struggles to understand if one can retain anything valuable from a discarded past.

A nameless fear would assail me from time to time. At first, it seemed to come over me without warning from the shadows around me, and I would gasp at its unexpectedness. Later, however, when the experience had become more familiar to me, my heart would readily succumb—or perhaps respond—to it; and I would begin to wonder if this fear had not always been in some hidden corner of my heart, ever since I was born. I would then ask myself whether I had not lost my sanity. But I had no desire to go to a doctor, or anyone else, for advice.

I felt very strongly the sinfulness of man. It was this feeling that sent me to K's grave every month, that made me take care of my mother-in-law in her illness and behave gently towards my wife. It was this sense of sin that led me to feel sometimes that I would welcome a flogging even at the hands of strangers. When this desire for punishment became particularly strong, I would begin to feel that it should come from myself, and not others. Then I would think of death. Killing myself seemed a just punishment. Finally, I decided to go on living as if I were dead. . . .

Then, at the height of the summer, Emperor Meiji passed away. I felt as though the spirit of the Meiji era had begun with the Emperor and had ended with him. I was overcome with the feeling that I and the others, who had been brought up in that era, were now left behind to live as anachronisms. I told my wife so. She laughed and refused to take me seriously. Then she said a curious thing, albeit in jest: "Well then, *junshi* is the solution to your problem." [1]

I had almost forgotten that there was such a word as "*junshi.*" It is not a word that one uses normally, and I suppose it had been banished to some remote corner of my memory. I turned to my wife, who had reminded me of its existence, and said, "I will commit *junshi* if you like; but in my case, it will be through loyalty to the spirit of the Meiji era." My remark was meant as a joke; but I did feel that the antiquated word had come to hold a new meaning for me.

A month passed. On the night of the Imperial Funeral I sat in my study and listened to the booming of the cannon. To me, it sounded like the last lament for the passing of an age.

Sensei is portrayed, along with the other major characters, as caught between different worlds and sets of values—between country and city, Japan and the West, traditional Japan and Modernity. In his living death, and perhaps in his eventual suicide, Sensei is portrayed as a modern everyman who finds only loneliness and alienation in the Meiji "heart of things."

The short novel, *So Long a Letter*, by Senegalese author Mariama Bâ, won the Noma prize in 1980 as best fiction in French written overseas (Bâ 1980, 88). Bâ is one of many contemporary African women writers who address issues of conflicting traditions, such as animism versus Islam or Christianity, monogamy versus polygamy and indigenous versus Europeanized values. The following excerpt is the conclusion of the long letter which the narrator, a recently widowed, educated mother of 12 is writing to her old friend who is divorced and has been living in America.

Why aren't your sons coming with you? Ah, their studies. . . .

So, then, will I see you tomorrow in a tailored suit or a long dress? I've taken a bet with Daba: tailored suit. Used to living far away, you will want—again. I have taken a bet with Daba—table, plate, chair, fork.

More convenient, you will say. But I will not let you have your way. I will spread out a mat. On it there will be the big, steaming bowl into which you will have to accept that other hands dip.

Beneath the shell that has hardened you over the years, beneath your skeptical pout, your easy carriage, perhaps I will feel you vibrate. I would so much like to hear you check or encourage my eagerness, just as you did before, and, as before, to see you take part in the search for a new way.

I warn you already, I have not given up wanting to refashion my life. Despite everything—disappointments and humiliations—hope still lives on within me. It

---

1. *Junshi*, even during Soseki's time, was a feudal term meaning "to follow one's lord to the grave."

is from the dirty and nauseating humus that the green plant sprouts into life, and I can feel new buds springing up in me.

The word 'happiness' does indeed have meaning, doesn't it? I shall go out in search of it. Too bad for me if once again I have to write you so long a letter. . . .

So Long a Letter engages many of the same questions of continuity and change that are raised in "The Waste Land" and *Kokoro*, but this time from the perspective of a contemporary African Muslim woman. The husbands of both the narrator and her friend had taken young second wives at the urging of an older generation. The narrator's daughters represent a hopeful vision of a future in which women and men are equal, and equally concerned about each other's happiness. The novel pushes students to probe beyond the superficial images of Islam and African culture so often found in the mass media.

The three-course concentration in international studies in the liberal arts curriculum, and especially in the TOP international program, is designed to lead students to explore issues of tradition and modernity as they arise in three different cultures. All three texts invite students to reflect on what is valuable from the past, what can be preserved, and how modernity challenges and perhaps destroys these traditions. At the end of the courses, we hope students come to a greater understanding of the complexity of different cultural perspectives and how our ways of thinking about our personal relationships are influenced by our cultural, as well as personal histories.

FINANCIAL SUPPORT

The progress made in internationalizing our campus would never have been possible without a series of grants which allowed for course and faculty development. An important step came when we received two grants from the National Endowment for the Humanities (NEH) to support faculty development for our Cultural Traditions course sequence. Cultural Traditions consists of two three-credit, interdisciplinary humanities courses, designed to give our students a strong foundation in the humanities by challenging them to read and analyze primary texts, including works of art and music, and providing them with the broad cultural/historical framework essential for the integration of new knowledge. Humanities 101 begins with antiquity and ends with the Renaissance. Humanities 102 includes the Enlightenment, romanticism, and the twentieth century. While the main focus of these courses is on Western cultural traditions, during a fourth unit of about three weeks, students read primary texts drawn from a non-Western based culture. The non-Western material is thematically connected to the European-based texts and integrated into the course structure.

In 1992, the NEH granted funds to the college for the first Cultural

Traditions Project, with the purpose to improve the faculty's ability to teach Humanities 101. The centerpiece of the two-year project was a summer seminar for 18 faculty, with the focus "Concepts of Duty in the Ancient World: Western and Chinese." Each faculty participant developed an annotated syllabus detailing how he or she planned to infuse global, and especially Chinese, material into the course. The college received a second NEH grant in 1994 for Humanities 102. The focus was on teaching Western material from the seventeenth to nineteenth centuries, and two non-Western areas: Tokugawa, Japan, and contemporary Latin America. An NEH institutional seminar in 1994 dealt with "Conflicting Conceptions of 'Self and Other' in the West and Japan: The Early Seventeenth to the Early Nineteenth Centuries." An on-going series of lectures and workshops by visiting scholars, initially funded by the NEH and currently funded by the college, allowed for a semester of activities in 1995 on African materials and topics. Finally, research begun by college faculty as a result of these seminars has been presented in both annual one-day conferences at the college in the spring of 1995 and 1996 ("Evolving Traditions in Cultural Traditions") and in regional and national conferences.

While the cultural traditions projects allowed a significant number of faculty to infuse Chinese, Japanese, African, and Latin American material into the cultural traditions and other courses, the approval of the new liberal arts curriculum and its International Studies Option required both a more extensive infusion of international material throughout the curriculum and the formulation of new area studies courses for the course concentration "mini-majors." In addition, although the college had a quite extensive selection of foreign language courses, enrollment in many languages had been declining, extensive use of multimedia technology was not in place, and first- and second-year courses in Japanese and Chinese did not exist.

To meet these needs, the college was awarded a Title VI Grant from the Department of Education. This grant, which began in 1996 and is expected to run through 1998, will allow us to address the needs of our new liberal arts curriculum. Two groups of faculty (Course Development Faculty) have been chosen to design new area studies courses in Far East Asian and African studies. These courses will be in a variety of departments in both the humanities and social sciences. Simultaneously, two other teams (Course Infusion Faculty) will be working on material which will be integrated into a wide variety of courses throughout the curriculum. All the project faculty will participate at various points in two six-week summer seminars in 1997 and 1998 on topics and texts from East Asia and Africa. Foreign language needs of the curriculum will be addressed through design of a new first-year Japanese course sequence, development of French language, African material, and a series of workshops on using multimedia technology to teach foreign languages.

Concurrently, with the first year of the Title VI grant, a related faculty seminar in Japanese literature and culture has involved an additional 25 faculty. This seminar is funded by The Japan Foundation, under the aegis of Columbia University. Participants have developed sample assignments based on seminar materials and incorporated them into courses at all levels, including remedial.

REACHING BEYOND THE CAMPUS

Finally, the college has been expanding the scope of international studies beyond the college community itself and into a regional, academic context. In October of 1996, Community College of Philadelphia hosted a two-day regional conference on "Asian Studies in the Undergraduate Curriculum." The college also established a regional resource center for Asian studies, which was inaugurated at the conference. The 1997 seminar on China and Japan may expand to a more regional focus, and funding is being pursued which would allow us, in conjunction with the East/West Center in Hawaii, to host a national conference on Asian and African relations.

These examples provide some illustrations of how our institution has used grant funding, both infusion and area studies approaches to course and faculty development, and an institutionalization of initiatives to move forward in international education. These grants have allowed faculty, with a very heavy teaching load, the time to update their knowledge in their disciplines and develop course modules in international studies. Through obtaining and realizing the objectives of earlier grants, the college has been able to "piggyback" grants, moving from a more general infusion approach, to development of more concentrated, sophomore-level area studies courses. And perhaps most significantly, grants and the overall process have helped build institutional and administrative support for global education, helping more at the college realize, as stated in the report on community colleges mentioned earlier, that "the 'community' identified in the mission statement no longer is confined to the limited geographical area" in which the college is physically located (Chase and Mahoney 1996, 5). Our commitment must be that we, as educators, serve a truly global community.

REFERENCES

Bâ, Mariama. 1980. *So Long a Letter.* Portsmouth, N.H.: Heinemann.
Chase, Audree M. and James R. Mahoney, eds. 1996. *Global Awareness in Community Colleges: A Report of a National Survey.* Washington, D.C.: American Association of Community Colleges.
Eliot, T. S. 1995. "The Waste Land." In *Western Literature in a World Context*, by Paul Davis, et al. Vol. 2. New York: St. Martin's Press.
Jameson, Fredric. 1993. Foreword to *Origins of Modern Japanese Literature*, by Karatani Kojin. Durham, N.C.: Duke University Press.
Johnston, Jr., Joseph S. and Richard J. Edelstein. 1993. *Beyond Borders: Profiles in*

International Education. Washington, D.C.: Association of American Colleges.
Soseki, Natsume. 1957. *Kokoro.* Translated by Edwin McClellan. Washington, D.C.: Regnery Gateway Press.

Chapter 15

A Transnational Model for Internationalizing the Curriculum

Michael Mooney, Takehiko Kawase, Michael Reardon, Frederick Nunn, and Ellen Mashiko

To internationalize the curriculum of an institution is a daunting task, but to do so in diverse institutions spanning two nations is even more formidable. Five institutions in the U.S.—Lewis and Clark College, Oregon State University, Pacific University, Portland State University, and the University of Oregon—and one in Japan, Waseda University, have been engaged in a bold transnational experiment since 1992.

The experiment involves the joint conceptualization, design, planning, teaching, assessment, and administration of an intensive, theme-focused, academic summer program. The program is geared to equivalent numbers of undergraduate students enrolled in U.S. colleges and universities and at Waseda University, Tokyo, who have studied and lived together on the campus of Lewis and Clark College in Portland, Oregon, the host institution.

Student and faculty assessments of the 1992-1995 programs have attested to the feasibility, appropriateness, and interest in a number of components: a comprehensive academic program that integrates courses designed to address a theme from transcultural and transdisciplinary perspectives; adjunct language courses (Japanese and English); extracurricular activities; and a shared living experience. The program assessments have also identified the benefits and challenges that accrue when binational teams of faculty jointly develop and teach courses.

BACKGROUND

During the last 50 years, three shifts in perspective have occurred that have a bearing on the field of international studies. In the post-World

War II period, foreigners, especially those destined for leadership positions in their home countries, sought to become familiar with American values, principles, and customs. Then the post-Sputnik era brought an awareness on the part of Americans, especially those headed for international business and government careers, of the languages and cultures of other countries, notably Europe and East Asia. Finally, in the current post-Cold War period, Americans and non-Americans alike consider it invaluable to know one another's languages, political forms, social, and economic systems, and to appreciate similarities and differences.

Over the same half-century, Japan and its system of education have also undergone substantial change. These changes have included rebuilding a system of education based on a reconstituted educational structure, the "massification" of higher education to meet the needs of a rapidly developing economy, and reforming education, particularly in the higher education sector, to meet global challenges. The current challenges encountered by the Japanese in higher education and the effects of the post-Cold War period in the United States have many similarities.

CONTEXT

Waseda University and a consortium of state and private institutions in Oregon embarked upon a joint exploration of new and yet-to-be-defined approaches to internationalizing their respective institutions in 1991. This search was grounded in a quarter-century-long relationship between the Oregon State System of Higher Education (OSSHE) and Waseda University, a cooperative endeavor of educational, business, and government leaders in Oregon, and an institutional commitment by Waseda to move beyond traditional, bilateral exchanges of students and faculty. The interests of all parties converged, albeit in different but complementary ways, and paved the way for a bold experiment to test the concepts that emerged during numerous meetings.

PARADIGM SHIFT

During this process, numerous conceptual changes occurred at various levels, including shifts from:

- a bilateral to a multilateral mode,
- a binational to a transnational approach,
- a student-focused to a student/faculty/administrator/staff perspective,
- a discipline-bound curriculum to a transdisciplinary, theme-focused curriculum,
- international exchange to an international education emphasis,
- international studies to an internationalization of general education, and
- meeting the needs of foreign language and area studies majors to offering a substantive academic program to students majoring in any field.

At the core of the still-evolving paradigm are emphases upon academic and programmatic matters rather than bricks and mortar; joint planning, teaching, administering, and assessment, rather than reliance on the receiving or host institution; mutual beneficiality rather than acquiescing to the needs of a single institution; and concern for pedagogy, curriculum, and staff development.

Two major shifts at Waseda University must be noted. First is the exploration and development of a university-wide undergraduate curriculum that bridges its nine undergraduate schools and brings together both students and faculty from these independent academic units. Second is the integration of foreign language and general education courses which have traditionally been separated.

PROGRAM DESIGN

The Waseda/Oregon Summer Programs to date have been designed to reflect the conceptual framework developed by the participating institutions and to fit home institution curricula. For example, the development of this joint program has been integrated into the extensive revision of both general education and international studies curricula at Portland State University. Furthermore, the interdisciplinary nature of the program permits faculty with an interest and commitment to being directly involved in a unique educational experiment to teach in the program irrespective of their fields of specialization.

PRACTICAL ISSUES

The development of this fundamentally and thoroughly joint program has required the acknowledgment of differences in administrative practices and style, as well as in the pace of program development and operation. What has emerged is a hybrid organizational structure and operational style which has been occasionally more time-consuming and required more thought and consideration than a program based in a single institution. However, despite differences in language skills, international experience, and customs and style, an immeasurable increase in shared values among students, faculty, and staff have developed and been sustained well beyond the period of program participation. It appears that the key has been to discover how to tap commitment and learning capacity at all levels and among all participants.

NEXT STEPS

A shared agenda has emerged for the near- and long-term future, including:

- translating the intensive, academic summer program into one which is operational throughout the calendar year,
- moving from a binational to multinational mode by including institutions from countries other than the U.S. and Japan,
- planning for the program to be conducted not only in the U.S. but also in Japan and other countries, and [1]
- conducting conceptually based, systematic, analytical research of the summer programs offered to date and subsequent programs.

---

1. The 1997 Waseda/Oregon Summer Program will be offered on the Waseda University campus in Tokyo for four weeks and on the Lewis and Clark College campus in Portland for five weeks, allowing participating students to experience both U.S. and Japanese learning and cultural environments, and to earn 12 to 15 semester credits.

Appendix A

A Sample Course Syllabus: Cultural Encounters: Conquest, Colonialism, Travel, Anthropology, and the "Writing" of Culture

Frances E. Mascia-Lees

REQUIRED TEXTS

Cartwright, Justin. *Masai Dreaming*. New York: Random House, 1995.
Mitchell, Timothy. *Colonising Egypt*. New York: Cambridge University Press, 1988.
Todorov, Tzvetan. *The Conquest of America*. New York: Harper & Row, 1984.
Tsing, Anna Lowenhaupt. *In the Realm of the Diamond Queen: Marginality in an Out-of-the-Way Place*. Princeton, N.J.: Princeton University Press, 1993.
Wolf, Margery. *A Thrice Told Tale: Feminism, Postmodernism, and Ethnographic Responsibility*. Stanford, Ca.: Stanford University Press, 1992.

COURSE DESCRIPTION

Individuals' experiences of foreign cultures are shaped by often unrecognized assumptions and traditions of interpretation which develop out of the history of contact between the culture of the traveler and the destination. Such interactions, while various, fall into types associated with particular genres of representation. This interdisciplinary course draws on current work in anthropology and cultural studies to explore some of the primary ways in which people from the West have encountered non-Western peoples. The experiences of travelers, whether explorer, adventurer, conquistador, missionary, colonial administrator, or anthropologist are analyzed in terms of their relationship to conventional forms of cultural representation, whether travel writing, report, novel, short story, film, or ethnography. Each type of cultural encounter is explored theoretically and through a case study that gives it concrete form.

COURSE OBJECTIVES

The objectives of this course are:

- to introduce the student to the significance of different types of cross-cultural encounters, including their history, politics, and ethicality;
- to provide the student with the kind of theoretical basis that will allow him or her to think critically about the relationship of power, knowledge, and representation in the construction of cultural encounters;
- to explore types of cultural description in order to provide the student with a variety of ways for thinking about and communicating personal experiences of another culture;
- to help the student uncover some of the assumptions about other cultures that have hindered or facilitated cross-cultural understanding;
- to introduce the student to some of the fundamental techniques of anthropological fieldwork and to provide experience in undertaking a short ethnographic study; and
- to help prepare the student planning to travel to and study in another culture to interrogate his or her own cultural assumptions.

COURSE REQUIREMENTS

Participation in Discussions of the Reading   **10% of grade**

Five Exercises   **30% of grade**

Students will be asked to complete the five short exercises described in the course outline.

Midterm Essay   **10% of grade**

The class will be asked to write a three-page essay on one of several topics to be distributed in class. This will be used to assess student's ability to compare, contrast, and analyze the ideas presented in the reading from the first part of this course.

Three Writing Assignments: Travel Writing, Short Story, and Ethnography   **40% of grade**

These are pieces of writing that will be worked on in small groups in class, written outside of class, and then read and discussed in class. Grades will be based on the quality of writing, the student's ability to integrate ideas discussed in class about these forms of representation, and on the quality of his or her participation in the constructive critique of other classmates' writing.

Final Essay   **10% of grade**

The student will be required to write a two-page analysis of the work done for this course, focusing especially on the three writing assignments to assess how genre affected, facilitated, and/or constrained the way in which a person's experiences of cultural encounters could be represented.

SCHEDULE OF CLASSES

Readings listed below that are on reserve are followed by (r).

I. Voyage, "Discovery," Conquest, and Colonialism

Tues.   **Introduction and Course Requirements**

Thurs.   **Voyage, "Discovery," and the Ethical Problems of Cultural Contact**
           "Some Remarks on Contact Among Cultures," by Tzvetan Todorov (r)
           "The Collection of the World: Accounts of Voyages from the Sixteenth to the Eighteenth Centuries," by Daniel Defert (r)
           Chapter 1 in *The Conquest of America*, by Tzvetan Todorov: "Discovery"

Tues.   **Conquest and Missionization as Cultural Encounter**
           Video: *The Mission*

Thurs.   **Conquest as Cultural Encounter: A Semiotic Analysis**
           Chapters 2 and 3 in *The Conquest of America*, by Tzvetan Todorov: "Love" and "Knowledge"
           "The Wrong Causes for the Wrong Reasons," by Tzvetan Todorov (r)

Tues.   **The Representation of Missionization**
           Exercise #1 Due: A two- to three-page analysis of missionization as a cultural encounter as represented in *The Mission*, that draws on (1) Todorov, especially Chapter 4 of *The Conquest of America*, but his other chapters and articles, as well, (2) the excerpt from "Colonial Governmentality and Conversion," by Nicholas Thomas (r), and (3) "Missionary Work as a Cultural Relationship: The French in Canada" (r).

Thurs.   **Colonialism as Cultural Encounter: A Foucauldian Approach**
           Chapters 1-4 in *Colonising Egypt*, by Timothy Mitchell

Tues.   **Colonialism as Cultural Encounter: Beyond Foucault**
           Chapters 3-6 in *Colonising Egypt*, by Timothy Mitchell

Thurs. **Tropes of Colonial Discourse**
Exercise #2 Due: Choose one of David Spurr's 11 "tropes of colonial discourse" (Chapters 1-11 correspond to his 11 tropes) from *The Rhetoric of Empire* (r) and find an instance of its use. Choose an example other than the ones Spurr himself uses. Then write a two- to three-page analysis of your choice of an instance of one of these tropes in light of the reading for this, and the last, class.

Tues. **Anthropology, Colonialism, and Colonial Discourse**
"Introduction," by Nicholas Thomas (r)
"From Present to Past: The Politics of Colonial Studies," by Nicholas Thomas (r)
"Fieldwork in Common Places," by Mary Louise Pratt (r)
"Slide Show: Evans-Pritchard's African Transparencies," by Clifford Geertz (r)
"Two European Images of Non-European Rule," by Talal Asad (r)

II. Travel and Tourism

Thurs. **The Traveler versus the Tourist**
Videos: *The Sheltering Sky* and *The Accidental Tourist*

MIDTERM ESSAY DUE

Tues. **Travel as Cultural Politics**
"For a History of Travel," by Eric Leed (r)
"The Mind of the Modern Traveler," by Eric Leed (r)
Exercise #3 Due: A two- to three-page comparison of travel versus tourism as metaphors for human interaction, as represented in *The Sheltering Sky* and *The Accidental Tourist*, and in light of the reading for this class.

Thurs. **Travel Writing: Group Work** (in class)
"Travel," by Rand Richards Cooper (r)
"Love at First Sight" from *Baghdad Without a Map*, by Tony Horwitz (r)
    Short excerpts from:
        Incidents of Travel in the Yucatan, by John L. Stephens (r)
        The Great Railway Bazaar, by Paul Theroux (r)

Tues. **Tourism's Impact**
Videos: *60 Minutes* segment on tourism and *The Toured: The Other Side of Tourism in Barbados*

Thurs. **The Politics of International Tourism**
"On the Beach: Sexism and Tourism," by Cynthia Enloe (r)

"Fucking Tourists," by B. Bowman (r)
"The Tourist Gaze" and "Cultural Changes and the Restructuring of Tourism," by John Urry (r)
"The British Virgin Islands as Nation and Desti-Nation," by Colleen Cohen and Fran Mascia-Lees (r)

Tues.   **Travel Writing**
Writing Assignment #1 Due: See handout for details. You will be asked to present these in class.

Thurs.   **Tourism: Brochures, Postcards, Photographs, and Souvenirs**
"Marketing the Parks," by Stephen Fjellman (r)
"The Locke Case," by Dean MacCannell (r)
"Travels in Hyperreality," by Umberto Eco (r)
"Secrets of the Interior," by M. H. Dunlop (r)
Exercise #4 Due: A two- to three-page deconstruction of your own souvenirs, postcards, and/or photographs in terms of yourself as a tourist in light of the reading.

III. Border Crossings in Fiction and Film

Tues.   **Cultural Encounter in Short Story: Group Work** (in class)
"A Wife's Story," by Bharati Mukherjee (r) (short story)
"Sleeping Beauty," by Gabriel García Márquez (r) (short story)
"Never Marry a Mexican," by Sandra Cisneros (r) (short story)
"The Harmony of Spheres," by Salman Rushdie (r) (short story)

Thurs.   **Border Crossings**
Video: *Mississippi Masala*
Start reading *Masai Dreaming*, by Justin Cartwright.

Tues.   **Cultural Encounter in Short Story**
Writing Assignment #2 Due: See handout for details. The first half of the class will be asked to read their stories in class. Continue reading *Masai Dreaming*, by Justin Cartwright.

Thurs.   **Border Crossing: Anthropology, Film, and Literature**
Writing Assignment #2 Due: See handout for details. The second half of the class will be asked to read their stories in class. Continue reading *Masai Dreaming*, by Justin Cartwright.

IV. Writing Culture: Anthropology and the New Ethnography

Tues.   **Ethnography in Fiction and Reality**
In the Realm of the Diamond Queen, by Anna Tsing

Finish reading *Masai Dreaming*, by Justin Cartwright.

Exercise #5 Due: A one- to two-page analysis of the following: *Masai Dreaming* critiques anthropology as a cultural encounter and its relationship to the popular representation of non-Western peoples, particularly in film. Yet, it is itself a conveyor of such depictions. *In the Realm of the Diamond Queen*, by contrast, presents an account of actual anthropological fieldwork. In an attempt to get at some of the assumptions underlying fieldwork, as well as some of its strengths and weaknesses as a type of cultural encounter, compare and contrast the image of anthropology in these two books, as well as its relationship to cross-cultural representation.

Two weeks **Independent Field Projects**
A Thrice-Told Tale, by Margery Wolf, all
You will be expected to be working on your independent field projects during this time. There will be no regular class. You are expected to do fieldwork for a minimum of **five hours** during this period and to document it with field notes.

Thurs. **Writing Ethnography: Group Work** (in class)
(Bring a draft of your ethnography to class.)

Tues. **Ethnography**
Writing Assignment #3 and Final Essay Due: You will be asked to present these in class.

COURSE DIMENSIONS: THE ETHICS, HISTORY, AND POLITICS OF CULTURAL ENCOUNTERS

I. Ethical and Historical Dimensions

Reading: "Some Remarks on Contact Among Cultures," by Tzvetan Todorov:

- What should your interactions with other cultures be like?
- What are the underlying assumptions that have governed the answers to this question at different historical moments?
- How does your understanding of these assumptions for any particular moment in the past affect how you might answer this question for the present?
- What are the current ways in which the ethical questions concerning cultural encounters are being framed and addressed?

II. Political Dimensions

Reading: "The Collection of the World: Accounts of Voyages from the

Sixteenth to the Eighteenth Centuries," by Daniel Defert

A. Power and Knowledge

• What is the relationship of cultural encounters to power and domination?
  One focus: Foucault's concept of the power/knowledge nexus: Power and knowledge are never separable because within each society there is a "regime of truth" with its own mechanisms for producing "truth." Truth is never outside of power. Mechanisms for the production of truth include discourses and discursive practices. Discourse: Ways of speaking and clusters of nonverbal practices that maintain relations and patterns of dominance in institutions and social processes.
• What happens when the "other" becomes an object of knowledge?
• How is it constituted as one?
• How is it brought into view?

B. Power and Representation

• What is the relationship of power and domination to genres of representation?
• What are the organizational schemes of types of texts?
• What kind of observations do they produce?
• To what tactics of domination do they correspond?

The student is asked to dissect examples of travel writing, fiction, and ethnography, to experiment with writing a personal experience of a cultural encounter using each of these forms, and to think self-reflexively about the relationship of form to content.

C. Power and Interpretation

Reading: Chapter 1 in *The Conquest of America* by Tzvetan Todorov: "Discovery"

• What is the relationship of power and domination to modes of interpretation?
• Todorov, using a semiotic approach, asks what is Columbus' interpretive strategy? What is Cortes'?
• What are our own interpretive systems?
• How can we discover them?

WRITING ASSIGNMENTS

Writing Assignment #1: Travel Writing

Purpose of Assignment: To encourage the student to think about travel as a culturally constructed experience and its relationship to travel writing as a genre of representation. (Travel writing continues to be a very popular form through which individuals in the United States come to find out about other ways of life. Just check out any popular bookstore and compare the travel section to the one containing ethnographies, for example).

Reading Assignment: The following pieces are to be read for discussion in class and then applied to this assignment:

Eric Leeds's "The Mind of the Modern Traveler" and "For a History of Travel"

Rand Richards Cooper's "Travel"

Paul Theroux's *The Great Railway Bazaar* (excerpt)

Tony Horwitz's "Love at First Sight" from *Baghdad Without a Map*

John Stephens's *Incidents of Travel in the Yucatan* (excerpt)

Writing Assignment: Write a three- to four-page description of a travel experience that draws on your understanding of travel as a mode of cultural encounter, as analyzed by Leeds. Your account should integrate ideas about travel writing from Cooper's "Travel," and should emulate in some way the travel writing of Theroux, Horwitz, or Stephens.

In-Class Assignment: After working in small groups, students will be asked to come to class prepared to read their travel accounts to the class. The class will then be asked to discuss what seems to make the piece an example of travel writing and in what ways it might be strengthened as a travel account. Student input is expected, but it should always be in the spirit of constructive feedback.

Writing Assignment #2: Short Story

Purpose of Assignment: To encourage the student to think about the experience of cultural identity as one necessarily constructed in cultural encounter. Each of the authors you'll read comes from a background other than the dominant Western one, but has been affected by this larger cultural context. Reading them should help you think about how your own cultural identity is a product of cultural encounter, even if in nonobvious ways.

Reading Assignment: The following short stories are to be read for discussion in small groups and then applied to this assignment:

"A Wife's Story," by Bharati Mukherjee

"Sleeping Beauty," by Gabriel García Márquez

"Never Marry a Mexican," by Sandra Cisneros

"The Harmony of Spheres," by Salman Rushdie

Writing Assignment: Write a three- to four-page short story that captures the nuances of a cultural identity constructed through cultural interaction. The story should be written in the style of Mukherjee, Márquez, Cisneros, or Rushdie.

In-Class Assignment: After working in small groups, students will be asked to come to class prepared to read their short stories to the class. The class will then be asked to discuss the piece in terms of its success as a description of a cultural encounter that captures the interaction in ways perhaps unique to fiction. Students will also be asked to offer suggestions about the ways the story might be strengthened in this regard. Input is expected, but it should always be in the spirit of constructive feedback.

Writing Assignment #3: Short Ethnography

Purpose of Assignment: To introduce the student to some of the fundamental techniques of anthropological investigation and to give them practice with both participant observation and the writing of ethnography. You will be encouraged to think critically about ethnography as a genre of cultural representation.

Reading Assignment: The following books are to be read for discussion in class and then applied to this assignment:

Masai Dreaming, by Justin Cartwright

In the Realm of the Diamond Queen, by Anna Tsing

A Thrice-Told Tale: Feminism, Postmodernism, and Ethnographic Responsibility, by Margery Wolf

Writing Assignment: Write a three- to four-page ethnography based on your five hours of ethnographic fieldwork that draws on insights about ethnography gained from our discussion of *Masai Dreaming* and *In the Realm of the Diamond Queen.* Travel should figure into your account in some way. So, for example, you might use it metaphorically and theoretically as Tsing does, or you might actually focus on travelers of some sort, as both Tsing and Cartwright do.

Independent Project and In-Class Assignment: For two weeks, the student will be expected to complete at least five hours of anthropological fieldwork, including the taking of field notes. Based on these, you will be asked to write a short ethnography, a draft of which you will work on in small groups. When class resumes, the student should come prepared to read his or her final draft.

The class will then be asked to discuss the piece in terms of its success as a description of a cultural phenomenon that captures it in ways characteristic of ethnography. Students will be asked to offer suggestions about the ways the piece might be strengthened in this regard. Input is expected, but it should always be in the spirit of constructive feedback.

Midterm Essays

Choose **one** of the following essays and respond to it in a short paper, no longer than three pages:

1) Mitchell's analysis of the nineteenth-century colonization of Egypt represents a Foucauldian analysis, while Todorov's analysis of the sixteenth-century conquest and subsequent colonization of Mexico is semiotic. Write an essay that identifies and analyzes the characteristics of these two approaches, compares them, and assesses their adequacy as explanatory models. It should be well-substantiated

with concrete examples from the texts.

2) Both *Colonising Egypt* and the articles from the class on "Colonial Discourse in Anthropology" focus on the relationship among power, knowledge, and representation. Drawing on our discussions of these texts and Spurr's *Rhetoric of Empire*, characterize, analyze, compare, and contrast colonial discourse outside of anthropology and within it. Be specific about what constitutes these discourses (draw particularly on the articles by Geertz, Pratt, and Asad for your characterization of colonial discourse in anthropology). What accounts for the similarities? The differences? Be specific and use concrete examples from the reading to illustrate your points.

Final Essay

Focusing on the three creative writing assignments you've done for this course, and drawing on Wolf and the articles read in the first part of this course, write a two- to three-page self-reflexive essay that analyzes how genre affected, facilitated, and/or constrained the way in which you could represent your experience of another culture.

QUESTIONS FOR DISCUSSION

Ethical and Political Issues in Cultural Encounters

The purpose of this reading is to prompt you to:

a) grapple with some of the ethical issues involved in cultural encounters,
b) investigate the relationship of power and domination to the process of interpretation that lies at the basis of cultural encounters, and
c) think about how historical political interactions between Western and non-Western societies may continue to affect your own interactions in another culture.

Keep the questions below in mind as you read:

"Some Remarks on Contact Among Cultures," by Tzvetan Todorov
"The Wrong Causes for the Wrong Reasons," by Tzvetan Todorov
"The Collection of the World: Accounts of Voyages from the Sixteenth to the Eighteenth Centuries," by Daniel Defert
The Conquest of America, by Tzvetan Todorov, Chapters 1 and 2

• What are some underlying assumptions that have governed the interactions of people from the West with non-Western peoples historically?
• How might your understanding of these assumptions for any particular moment in the past affect your response to this question in the present?
• What are some current ways in which the ethical questions concerning cultural encounters are being framed and addressed?
• What happens when the "other" becomes an object of knowledge? How has it

been constituted as one in the past, according to Defert? How does it continue
to be constituted as one today?
- According to Todorov, what was Columbus' interpretive strategy and what was
it based on? What was Montezuma's interpretive strategy?

Colonialism as Cultural Encounter

The purpose of this reading is to get you to think about how we might
theorize the relationship of colonial power to cultural encounter.

Keep the questions below in mind as you read Timothy Mitchell's
Colonising Egypt:

Mitchell's Argument:

- How, according to Mitchell, does one develop the power to colonize?
- What is the nature of colonial power, according to him?
- What are the particular forms of power he describes as part of the colonizing
process in Egypt? How do they work? To what are they related?
- What is the relationship between power and representation in this colonial
context?

Mitchell's Approach:

- What are the assumptions underlying Mitchell's argument about the nature of
colonial power?
- How would you characterize his approach? Give specific examples.
- What are the strengths and weaknesses of this approach in terms of understanding
colonization as a cultural encounter?

Anthropology, Colonialism, and Colonial Discourse

The purpose of this reading is to focus your attention on the relationship
of power to modes of investigation and genres of representation.

Keep the questions below in mind as you read the articles assigned for
class:
"Introduction," by Nicholas Thomas (r)
"From Present to Past: The Politics of Colonial Studies," by Nicholas
Thomas (r)
"Fieldwork in Common Places," by Mary Louise Pratt (r)
"Slide Show: Evans-Pritchard's African Transparencies," by Clifford
Geertz (r)
"Two European Images of Non-European Rule," by Talal Asad (r)

- According to these authors, to what extent did disciplines like anthropology
inform and legitimize colonial rule?
- How, according to each author, did this occur?
- What are the similarities among the articles in terms of how they respond to

these questions? The differences? What is significant about the similarities and differences in terms of understanding the relationship of anthropology to colonialism?

- According to each author, what are the relationships among colonialism, travel, and anthropology? What are the relationships among governmental documents, travel writing, and ethnography?
- What is the relationship of forms of ethnographic writing (the tropes, images, rhetorical styles, etc.) to the particular people being written about, the modes of interpretation and models of behavior embedded in historical circumstances, and the larger assumptions about knowledge underlying ethnographic accounts?
- How does each author, in one way or another, demonstrate Nicholas Thomas's claim in his "Introduction" to *Colonialism's Culture* that "colonialism consists not only of political and economic relations legitimized through discourses of racism, but also of cultural processes whose ideologies are imagined"? From what source do these imaginings spring, according to each author?

The Politics of International Tourism

Keep the question below in mind as you read the articles assigned for class:

"On the Beach: Sexism and Tourism," by Cynthia Enloe

"Fucking Tourists," by B. Bowman

"The Tourist Gaze," by John Urry

"The British Virgin Islands as Nation and Desti-Nation," by Colleen Cohen and Fran Mascia-Lees

- It is not uncommon for writers to think of tourism as a reenactment of the traditional power roles of colonialism. Thus, tourism is often characterized as little more than a form of neocolonialism in which the tourists from the dominant culture are exploiters of the helpless inhabitants of the tourist site. Using ideas from each of the articles, dispute this assertion paying particular attention to the complex power relations that are at play in tourism, the role gender plays in the tourist encounter, and the relationship of tourism to cultural identity.

Appendix B

Federal Funding Opportunities in Foreign Languages, Area Studies, and International Studies

1. **National Resource Centers and Fellowships Program for Language and Area Studies**
   ED—CIE (84.015)
   (202) 708-7283

   Supports centers and graduate fellowships in modern foreign language training, and area and international studies.

2. **Language Resource Centers**
   ED—CIE (84.229)
   deadline—March 1
   (202) 708-8763

   Funds research, material development and testing, proficiency training, curriculum and faculty development, of foreign language instruction at university language resource centers.

3. **Undergraduate International Studies and Foreign Language Program**
   ED—CIE (84.016)
   deadline—November 2 annually
   (202) 708-9293

   Can fund curriculum and faculty development, library acquisitions, linkages with overseas institutions, lecture series, consultants, short-

---

The information in Appendix B is deemed reliable, but not legally binding.

term faculty activities abroad. Cannot fund ongoing activities or student activities.

4. **International Research and Studies Program**
   ED—CIE (84.017)
   deadline—November 2 annually
   (202) 708-7283

   Funds research-oriented activities related to needs assessment, effectiveness of teaching methodology, evaluation, and development of specialized materials with respect to foreign language and area studies training.

5. **Business & International Education Program**
   ED—CIE (84.153A)
   deadline—November 9
   (202) 708-7283

   Fifty-fifty matching grants to enhance international business education programs for IHEs in agreements with business enterprises, trade organizations, or associations engaged in international economic activities.

6. **Fulbright-Hays Programs**
   Council for International Exchange of Scholars (CIES)
   (202) 686-7866

   A number of F-H Programs in most disciplines & locations including:

   a. *Fulbright Scholar Program*—Research, Lecturing, combined RIL, Junior R or L, Travel-Only for U.S. citizens.
   deadline—August 1
   b. *Scholar-in-Residence Program*—For one- or two-semester visits for scholars from abroad.
   deadline—November 1
   c. *Visiting Scholars & Occasional Lecturers*—Short-term visits to U.S. IHEs by visiting Fulbright recipients from abroad. See directory.
   d. *Fellowships for College & University Administrators*—For U.S. administrators at U.K. institutions.

7. **Fulbright-Hays Faculty Research Abroad**
   ED—Center for International Education (CIE) (84.019)
   deadline—October 30
   (202) 708-7279

Supports faculty research and study abroad in modern foreign languages and area studies. Geographic priorities include Africa, Asia, Near East, Eastern Europe, Baltics, and new states of the FSU.

8. **Fulbright-Hays Doctoral Dissertation Research Abroad**
    ED—Center for International Education (CIE) (84.022)
    deadline—October 30
    (202) 708-9291

    Supports faculty research and study abroad in modern foreign languages and area studies. Same priorities as above.

9. **Fulbright-Hays Group Projects Abroad**
    ED—Center for International Education (CIE) (84.021)
    deadline—October 23
    (202) 708-8294

    Supports curriculum and faculty development in foreign languages and area studies through projects affiliated with institutions abroad. For FY 93 priority was elementary and secondary level. Geographic priorities vary over time.

10. **Fulbright-Hays Seminars Abroad**
    ED—Center for International Education (CIE) (84.018)
    deadline—November 9
    (202) 708-7292

    For individual faculty members in humanities and social sciences area studies to attend seminars abroad. Seminars vary annually, and from each other, in terms of specific subject matter, and may or may not be of interest to any individual faculty member.

11. **Institute of International Education (IIE)**
    deadline—October 23
    (212) 984-5329

    Grants for predoctoral study or research abroad.

12. **U.S. Institute of Peace**
    deadline—January 2
    (202) 429-3844

    Makes solicited and unsolicited grants for a broad range of projects in field of international peace and conflict resolution.

13. **International Research & Exchanges Board (IREX)**
    deadline—varied
    (202) 628-8188

    Multiple faculty and graduate student exchange and language training programs for those in the humanities and social sciences to travel to Central and Eastern Europe, the Baltics, states of the FSU, and Mongolia.

14. **USIA**
    deadline—varied

    Multiple exchange, research, and training programs between U.S. and foreign scholars.

15. **University Affiliations Program**
    USIA
    deadline—January 15
    (202) 619-5289, 4420

    Supports institutional partnerships between U.S. and foreign institutions with exchanges of faculty and staff. Geographic priorities vary. College could establish program with an overseas institution and focus on certain topics.

16. **Special Opportunities in Foreign Language Education**
    NEH—Education Programs
    deadline—March 15
    (202) 786-0373

    Aimed at improving foreign language instruction—particularly Russian, Japanese, Chinese, Arabic. Supports summer institutes for school teachers, strengthening undergraduate language programs, and special projects.

17. **NEH—Division of Fellowships & Seminars**
    deadline—varied
    (202) 786-0463

    Supports humanities through fellowships for college faculty, dissertation grants, study grants, summer seminars. Younger Scholar Awards for precollege seniors.

18. **NEH—Division of Research Programs**
    deadline—varied
    (202) 786-0200

Supports humanities through preparation for publication of editions and translations, reference materials, interpretive research, collaborative projects, and research conferences.

19. **NSF**
Basic research and science education in social sciences—linguistics.

20. **Committee on Scholarly Communication with the People's Republic of China**
deadline—varied
(202) 337-1250

Supports a variety of programs including: Research in China, China Conference Travel Grants, and Fellowships for Graduate Study in China.

21. **ACLS (American Council of Learned Societies)**
deadline—varied
(212) 697-1505

Major fellowships and grants for research and projects in all disciplines of the humanities and the humanities-related social sciences, including sabbatical support, travel to international meetings, area studies programs, and dissertation research.

22. **American Philosophical Society (APS)**
deadline—four times each year
104 S. 5th St., Philadelphia, PA 19106

Postdoctoral grants of up to $5,000 for research only in almost all scholarly fields.

Nota bene: Remember that deadline dates, priorities, addresses, and phone numbers frequently change. Check far in advance and obtain latest, up-to-date materials.

Appendix C

Metropolitan D.C. Potential Sources for Internships, 1996–1997: Associations and Agencies with International Contacts/Services/Divisions

America Air Museum in Britain
709 2nd Street, NE
(202) 543-4226

America-Mideast Educational and Training Service, Inc.
1730 M Street, NW
(202) 776-9600

American Academy for Liberal Education
1015 18th Street, NW
(202) 452-8611

American Advisory Group—Czechoslovakia
1511 K Street, NW
(202) 638-5505

American Arbitration Association
Office of National Affairs
1150 Connecticut Avenue, NW
(202) 296-8510

American Association for the Advancement of Science
Directorate for International Programs
1200 New York Avenue, NW
(202) 326-6650

American Association of University Women
International Fellowships
1111 16th Street, NW
(202) 785-7700

American Council on Education
International Education
1 Dupont Circle, NW
(202) 939-9313

Center for Applied Linguistics
1118 22nd Street, NW
(202) 429-9292

Center for Immigration Studies
1522 K Street, NW
(202) 466-8185

Institute for Asian Democracy
1518 K Street, NW
(202) 737-4101

Institute for Cooperation on Agriculture/ICA
1775 K Street, NW
(202) 458-3767

Institute for Foreign Policy Analysis, Inc.
1725 Desales Street, NW
(202) 463-7942

Institute for International Economics
11 Dupont Circle, NW
(202) 328-9000

Institute of International Education
1400 K Street, NW
(202) 898-0600

Institute for International Studies
1730 Rhode Island Avenue, NW
(202) 466-4406

Institute for the Study of Diplomacy
Diplomatic Associates
1316 36th Street, NW
(202) 965-5735

Institute for Women's Policy Research
1400 20th Street, NW
(202) 785-5100

Inter-American Bar Association
1211 Connecticut Avenue, NW
(202) 393-1217

Inter-American College of Physicians and Surgeons
Positions Exchange Program
1712 I Street, NW
(202) 467-4756

Inter-American Defense Board
Logistics and Special Studies Division
2600 16th Street, NW
(202) 939-6600

Inter-American Development Bank
Literacy Development
1300 New York Avenue, NW
(202) 623-1000

International Association for Continuing Education and Training
1200 19th Street, NW
(202) 857-1122

International Center for Information Technologies
727 15th Street, NW
(202) 639-8800

International Center for Language Studies, Inc.
727 15th Street, NW
(202) 639-8800

International Council of Museums
1225 I Street, NW
(202) 289-1818

International Council on Education for Teaching
2009 N. 14th Street, Suite 609
North Arlington, VA 22201
(703) 525-5253

International Institute for Strategic Studies
U.S. Committee
P.O Box 7692
McLean, VA 22106-7692
(703) 351-6812

International Policy Council on Agriculture and Trade
1616 P Street, NW
(202) 328-5056

International Student Exchange Program
1601 Connecticut Avenue, NW
(202) 667-8027

International Student House
1825 R Street, NW
(202) 232-4007

International Women's Forum
1826 Jefferson Place, NW
(202) 775-8917

John Snow, Inc.
Women's Literacy Initiative
The Seats Project
Family Planning Service Expansion & Technical Support
1616 N. Fort Myer Drive, 11th floor
Arlington, VA 22209
(703) 528-7474

Meridian International Center
Visitors Service
1630 Crescent Place, NW
(202) 939-5544

National Association for Women in Education
1325 18th Street, NW
(202) 659-9330

National Commission on Libraries and Information Science
1100 Connecticut Avenue, NW
(202) 606-9200

National Council on Disability
1331 F Street, NW
(202) 272-2004

National Institute for Literacy
800 Connecticut Avenue, NW
(202) 632-1500

United Nations Association of the USA
1010 Vermont Avenue, NW
(202) 347-5004

United Nations Association—National Capital Area
1319 18th Street, NW
(202) 785-2640

United Nations Information Center
1775 K Street, NW
(202) 331-8670

United States Institute of Peace
1550 M Street, NW
(202) 457-1700

The Washington International Studies Council
214 Massachusetts Avenue, NE
(202) 547-3275

Woodrow Wilson Center
1000 Jefferson Drive, SW
(202) 357-2429

Selected Bibliography

Adams, Maurianne, ed. "Promoting Diversity in College Classrooms: Innovative Responses for the Curriculum, Faculty, and Institutions." *New Directions for Teaching and Learning* 52. San Francisco: Jossey-Bass, 1992.

Adelman, Clifford, et al. "Building Communities of Civility and Respect." *Educational Review* (winter 1995).

Adler, Peter S. "The Transitional Experience: An Alternate View of Culture Shock." *The Journal of Humanistic Psychology* 15, no. 4 (fall 1975): 13-23.

Ahmed, Z. V. and F. B. Krohn. "The Symbiosis of Liberal Arts and International Business." *Journal of Education for Business* 69, no. 4 (1994): 199-203.

Aitches, Marian and Tom Hoemeke. "Education Abroad and International Exchange." In *Bridges to the Future Strategies for Internationalizing Higher Education,* edited by Charles B. Klasek. Carbondale, Ill.: Association of International Education Administrators; Southern Illinois University, 1992.

American Association for Higher Education. "What Research Says About Improving Undergraduate Education." *AAHE Bulletin* (1996): 5-8.

American Council of Education. *Educating Americans for a World in Flux: Ten Ground Rules for Internationalizing Higher Education.* Washington, D.C., 1995.

———. *Guidelines for College and University Linkages Abroad.* Washington, D.C., 1993.

———. *An International Visitor's Guide to the U.S. Higher Education.* Washington, D.C., 1992.

———. *Serving the World: International Activities of American Colleges and Universities.* Washington, D.C., 1992.

———. *Spreading the Word: Improving the Way We Teach Foreign Languages.* Washington, D.C., 1994.

———. *Spreading the Word II: Promising Developments for Undergraduates' Foreign Language Instruction.* Washington, D.C., 1996.

———. *What We Can't Say Can Hurt Us: A Call for Foreign Language Competence by the Year 2000.* Washington, D.C., 1989.

Arnum, Stephen. *International Education: What Is It? A Taxonomy of International Education at U.S. Universities.* New York: Council on International Educational Exchange, 1987.

Association of American Colleges. *Liberal Education, Special Edition 77*, no. 3 (1991).

Association of International Education Administrators. *Guidelines for International Education at U.S. Colleges and Universities.* Washington, D.C., n.d.

————. *A Research Agenda for the Internationalization of Higher Education in the United States.* Washington, D.C., 1995.

Audas, Millie C. "Comparing Policy Statements and Practices in the International Dimension of Selected Institutions of Higher Education, Part 1." *International Education Forum* (fall 1990): 59-73.

Boyer, E. L. "Making the Connections." In *Rethinking the Curriculum*, edited by Mary E. Clark and Sandra A. Wawrytko. New York: Greenwood Press, 1990.

Boyer, E. L. and A. Livine. *A Quest for Common Learning.* Princeton: Princeton University Press, 1981.

Brecht, Richard D. and A. Ronald Walton. "The Future Shape of Language Learning: The New World of Global Communication: Consequences for Higher Education and Beyond." In *Foreign Language Learning: The Journey of a Lifetime*, edited by Richard Donato and Robert M. Terry. Lincolnwood, Ill.: National Textbook Company, 1995.

————. *National Strategic Planning: The Less Commonly Taught Languages.* Washington, D.C.: National Foreign Language Center, 1993.

————. "Policy Issues, Foreign Language, and Study Abroad." *Annals of the American Academy of Political and Social Science* 532 (March 1994): 213-225.

Carlson, Jerry S., Barbara B. Burn, John Useem, and Davis Yachimowicz. *Study Abroad: The Experience of American Undergraduates.* Westport, Conn.: Greenwood Press, 1990.

Carnegie Endowment National Commission on America and the New World. *Changing Our Ways: America and the New World.* Washington, D.C.: The Brookings Institution, 1992.

Carnegie Foundation for the Advancement of Teaching. *The Academic Profession: An International Perspective.* Princeton: 1994.

Carter, Holly M. "Implementation of International Competence Strategies: Faculty." In *Bridges to the Future: Strategies for Internationalizing Higher Education*, edited by Charles B. Klasek. Carbondale, Ill: Association of International Education Administrators; Southern Illinois University, 1992.

Cerny, P. G. "Globalization and the Changing Logic of Collective Action." *International Organization* 49, no. 4 (1995): 595-625.

Cohen, Jean L. and Andrew Arato. *Civil Society and Political Theory.* Cambridge, Mass.: MIT Press, 1994.

Council on International Educational Exchange. *Educating for Global Competence (Report of the Advisory Group on International Educational Exchange).* New York, 1988.

Daly, Herman E. and John B. Cobb, Jr. *For the Common Good: Redirecting the Economy Toward Community, the Environment, and a Sustainable Future.* Boston: Beacon Press, 1989.

Davis, James R. *Interdisciplinary Courses and Team Teaching: New Arrangements for Learning.* Phoenix: ACE/Oryx, 1995.

Davis, John L. "Developing a Strategy for Internationalization Universities: Toward a Conceptual Framework." In *Bridges to the Future: Strategies for Internationalizing Higher Education*, edited by Charles Klasek. Carbondale, Ill.: Association of International Education Administrators; Southern Illinois University, 1992.

DeKeyser, Robert M. "Foreign Language Development During a Semester Abroad." In *Foreign Language Acquisition Research and the Classroom*, edited by Barbara F. Freed. Lexington, Mass.: D. C. Heath & Co., 1991.

El-Khawas, Elaine. *Campus Trends 1995: New Directions for Academic Programs.* Washington, D.C.: American Council on Higher Education, 1995.

———. "Toward a Global University: Status and Outlook in the United States," *Higher Education Management* 6, no. 1 (March, 1994): 90-98.

Engerman, David and Parker G. Marden. *In the International Interest: Contributions and Needs of America's International Liberal Arts Colleges.* Beloit, Wis.: International Liberal Arts Colleges, 1992.

Gaudiani, Claire L. "Area Studies for a Multicultural World Transition," *Northeast Conference Reports* (1992): 73-86.

———. "For a New World, a New Curriculum," *Educational Record* (winter 1994): 20-29.

———. "Global Social Development: Higher Education's Next Moral Commitment," *Educational Record* (winter 1995): 7-13.

Goodwin, Craufurd D. and Michael Nacht. *Abroad and Beyond: Patterns in American Overseas Education.* Cambridge, Mass.: Cambridge University Press, 1988.

———. *Missing the Boat: The Failure to Internationalize American Higher Education.* Cambridge, Mass.: Cambridge University Press, 1991.

Gore, Joan Elias. *Recommendations for On-Campus Efforts to Internationalize the Campus and the Curriculum.* New York: Council on International Educational Exchange, 1992.

Gorjanc, A. A. "One World, Two Spheres: International Majors at Williams Woods College." Paper presented at the Annual Eastern Michigan University Conference on Language and Communication for World Business and the Professions. Ypsilanti, Mich., April 1993.

Groennings, Sven and David S. Wiley, eds. *Group Portrait: Internationalizing the Disciplines.* New York: The American Forum, 1990.

Hanson, Katherine H. and Joel W. Meyerson. *International Challenges to American Colleges and Universities: Looking Ahead.* Washington, D.C.: American Council on Education Series on Higher Education, 1995.

Harari, Maurice. "Internationalization of the Curriculum." In *Bridges to the Future: Strategies for Internationalizing Higher Education*, edited by Charles B. Klasek. Carbondale, Ill.: Association of International Education Administrators; Southern Illinois University, 1992.

Harari, Maurice and Richard F. Reiff. "Halfway There: A View From the Bridge. A Model for Internationalizing." *International Educator* (spring 1993).

Heller, S. "Fifty-two Private Colleges Said to Assume Major International Affairs Role." *Chronicle of Higher Education* 37, no. 41 (1991): A14.

Hersh, R. H. "The Liberal Arts College: Alma Mater Endangered." *Change* 26, no. 6 (1994): 53-55.

Hoemeke, Thomas H. "Education for International Competence and Competitiveness: The Texan Response." *International Education Forum* (fall 1990): 74-85.

Hoffa, Bill. "E-Mail and Study Abroad: The Pros and Cons of Travel and Learning Cyberspace." *Transitions Abroad* (January/February 1996): 79-81.

————. "Know Your Enemy: Confronting the Case Against Study Abroad." *Transitions Abroad* (May/June 1996): 74-5.

Huebner, Tom. "A Framework for Investigating the Effectiveness of Study Abroad." In *Redefining the Boundaries of Language Study*, edited by Claire Kramsch. Boston: Heinle and Heinle (1995): 185-217.

Johnston, Jr., Joseph S. and Richard J. Edelstein. *Beyond Borders: Profiles in International Education*. Washington, D.C.: Association of American Colleges, 1993.

Katz, Joseph et al. *A New Vitality in General Education: Planning, Teaching, and Supporting Effective Liberal Learning*. Washington, D.C.: Association of American Colleges, 1988.

Kauffmann, Norman L., Judith N. Martin, and Henry D. Weaver. *Students Abroad: Strangers at Home*. Yarmouth, Maine: Intercultural Press, 1992.

Kawase, Takehiko. "Kyoiku no. Kokusaika to Kokusaika Kyouiku" (The Internationalization of Education and International Education), *Daigaku Jiho (Journal of the Japan Association of Private Colleges and Universities)* 43, no. 237 (July 1994): 92-101.

Kelleher, Ann, Janet E. Rasmussen, R. Lynn Kelley, Jane Margaret O'Brien, and Robert Crane. "The International Campus." Thematic issue of *Liberal Education* (November/December 1991).

Kerr, Clark, Peter A. Wollitzer, Stanislav P. Merkur'ev, William H. Allaway, and Neil J. Smelser. "Internationalizing Higher Education." Thematic issue of *American Behavioral Scientist* (September/October 1991).

Klasek, Charles B., ed. *Bridges to the Future: Strategies for Internationalizing Higher Education*. Carbondale, Ill: Association of International Education Administrators, 1992.

Kohls, L. Robert. *Survival Kit for Overseas Living*. Yarmouth, Maine: Intercultural Press, Inc., 1984.

Krajewski, L. A. and J. A. Patrick. "Developing and Implementing an International Studies Minor: A Liberal Arts-Business Administration Partnership." Paper presented at the Annual Eastern Michigan University Conference on Language and Communication for World Business and the Professions. Ypsilanti, Mich., April 1994.

Krueger, Merle and Frank Ryan, eds. *Language and Content: Discipline- and Content-Based Approaches in Language Study*. Lexington, Mass.: D. C. Heath, 1993.

Küng, Hans and Karl-Josef Kuschel. *A Global Ethic: The Declaration of the Parliament of the World's Religions*. New York: Continuum, 1993.

Lambert, Richard D. "International Studies and Education: The Current State of Affairs." *International Education Forum* (spring 1990): 1-8.

————. *International Studies and the Undergraduate*. Washington, D.C.: American Council on Education, 1989.

Lamson, Howard. "International Education and Liberal Learning," *Liberal Education* (winter 1995).

Levinson, Nanette S. and Minoru Asahi, "Cross-national Alliances and Interorganizational Learning."*Organizational Dynamics* 24, no. 2(autumn 1995): 50-63.

Lewis, J. G. and M. M. Roth. "International Business and Liberal Arts Education: Building a Better Mousetrap." Paper presented at the Annual Eastern

Michigan University Conference on Language and Communication for World Business and the Professions. Ypsilanti, Mich., April 1993.

Lombardi, John V. "America International: Colleges, Universities, and Global Education." *International Education Forum* (spring 1991): 1-8.

Marden, Parker G. and David C. Engerman, "In the International Interest: Liberal Arts Colleges Take the High Road," *Educational Record* 73, no. 2 (spring 1992): 42-46.

Moseley, Merritt, ed. *Asheville Institute on General Education, Proceedings.* Washington, D.C.: Association of American Colleges, June 7-12, 1991.

Omaggio, Alice C. *Teaching Language in Context: Proficiency-Oriented Instruction.* Boston: Heinle and Heinle, 1986.

Pickert, Sarah M. *Preparing for a Global Community: Achieving an International Perspective Higher Education.* ASHE-ERIC Higher Education Report No. 2. Washington D. C.: George Washington University, 1992.

Pickert, Sarah M. and Barbara Turlington. *Internationalizing the Undergraduate Curriculum: A Handbook for Campus Leaders.* Washington, D.C.: American Council on Education, 1992.

Proctor, Robert E. *Education's Great Amnesia: Reconsidering the Humanities from Petrarch to Freud, with a Curriculum for Today's Students.* Bloomington, Ind.: Indiana University Press, 1991.

―――. "Grounding International Studies in the Liberal Arts Tradition." *ADFL Bulletin* 27, no. 1 (fall 1995).

Savitt, William, ed. *Teaching Global Development: A Curriculum Guide.* Notre Dame, Ind.: Notre Dame, 1993.

Schechter, Michael G. "Internationalizing the Undergraduate Curriculum." *International Education Forum* (spring 1990): 14-20.

Scott, Robert A. "Campus Developments Response to the Challenges of Internationalization: The Case of Ramapo College, New Jersey." *Higher Education Management* 6, no. 1 (1994).

Steiner, G. *Language and Silence.* New York: Antheneum, 1967.

Study Commission on Global Education. *The United States Prepares for Its Future: Global Perspectives Education.* New York: Global Perspectives in Education, Inc., 1987.

Tonkin, Humphery and Jane Edwards. "Internationalizing the University: The Arduous Path to Euphoria." *Educational Record* (spring 1990).

Urch, George E. "Preparing for a Global Community: Achieving an International Perspective on Higher Education." *Comparative Education Review* (February 1994).

Useem, M. "Corporate Restructuring and Liberal Learning." *Liberal Education* 81, no. 1 (1995): 18-23.

Van Doren, M. *Liberal Education.* New York: Holt, 1943.

Vestal, Theodore M. *International Education: Its History and Promise for Today.* Westport, Conn.: Praeger, 1994.

Wright, Sheila. "Promoting Intellectual Development During the Freshman Year." *Journal of the Freshman Year Experience* 4, no. 2 (1992): 23-39.

Index

About the Contributors

SUSAN COLEMAN is director of the International Center at the University of Hartford in West Hartford, Connecticut. She is also an assistant professor of finance in the Barney School of Business.

CLAIRE L. GAUDIANI is president of Connecticut College in New London, Connecticut. A professor of French, she lead the college in creating The Toor Cummings Center for International Studies in the Liberal Arts, as well as forged international teaching/studying initiatives. She is a founder of the Rockefeller Foundation-National Endowment for the Humanities Fellowship Program for high school foreign language teachers.

JANE HORVATH is associate director of the All-University Curriculum at the University of Hartford in West Hartford, Connecticut. She is also an associate professor of economics in Hillyer College.

TAKEHIKO KAWASE is dean of the International Division at Waseda University in Tokyo, Japan. He is also a professor of science and engineering.

MICHAEL KLINE is a professor of French at Dickinson College in Carlisle, Pennsylvania. He has also served as past director of Dickinson's program in Toulouse, France, and as past chair of the French and Italian Department.

MERLE KRUEGER is associate director of the Center for Language Studies at Brown University in Providence, Rhode Island. He is also an adjunct lecturer in the Department of German Studies.

JULIA A. KUSHIGIAN is director of The Toor Cummings Center for International Studies and the Liberal Arts at Connecticut College in New London, Connecticut. She is also an associate professor of Hispanic studies.

NANETTE S. LEVINSON is associate dean of the School of International Service at American University in Washington, D.C. She is also an associate professor of international relations.

DAVID A. J. MACEY is a professor of history and Cornelius V. Starr

Professor of Russian Studies at Middlebury College in Middlebury, Vermont. He is also director of both Russian and East European studies and the new international studies major, as well as director of Off-Campus Study.

M. KATHLEEN MAHNKE is an associate professor in the School of International Studies at St. Michael's College in Colchester, Vermont. She is also special assistant to the vice-president of academic affairs.

FRANCES E. MASCIA-LEES is a professor of anthropology and cultural studies at Simon's Rock College of Bard in Great Barrington, Massachusetts.

ELLEN MASHIKO is deputy executive director of the International Center at Waseda University in Tokyo, Japan. She is also the Overseas Projects Development Office administrator.

MICHAEL MOONEY is president of Lewis and Clark College in Portland, Oregon. He is also a professor of intellectual history.

FREDERICK NUNN is director of international affairs and the International Studies Program at Portland State University in Portland, Oregon. He is also a professor of history and international studies.

JOAN O'MARA is an associate professor of speech and drama in Hillyer College at the University of Hartford in West Hartford, Connecticut.

PENNY PARSEKIAN is a free-lance author and editor who lives in New London, Connecticut. She has written or edited 17 books on a wide range of subjects, as well as shorter pieces and articles for various clients including *The New York Times* and the National Georgraphic Society.

DAVID C. PREJSNAR is curriculum coordinator for international studies in the Liberal Arts Curriculum at the Community College of Philadelphia in Philadelphia, Pennsylvania. He is also project codirector of a Title VI Project, as well as a lecturer in humanities and religion in the History/Philosophy Department.

ROBERT E. PROCTOR is provost and dean of faculty at Connecticut College in New London, Connecticut. He is also the founding director of The Toor Cummings Center for International Studies, as well as a professor of Italian.

MICHAEL REARDON is vice-president for academic affairs and provost of Portland State University in Portland, Oregon. He is also a professor of history and humanities.

DENISE ROCHAT is an associate professor of French at Smith College in Northampton, Massachusetts. She is also a former director of the Smith College Junior Year for International Studies in Geneva.

KATHLEEN RUPRIGHT is chair of the Modern Languages Department and a professor of Spanish at St. Michael's College in Colchester, Vermont.

HARALD SANDSTROM is an associate professor of politics and government at the University of Hartford in West Hartford, Connecticut. He also coordinates majors in political economy and African American studies.

MARCIA SEABURY is an associate professor of English in Hillyer College

at the University of Hartford in West Hartford, Connecticut. She has just completed a three-year term as director of the All-University Curriculum.
BONNIE TANGALOS is dean of the School of International Studies at St. Michael's College in Colchester, Vermont.
ALISON TASCH is coordinator of the Liberal Arts Curriculum at the Community College of Philadelphia in Philadelphia, Pennsylvania. She is also an associate professor of English.
PETER S. THACHER is a World Resources Institute visiting fellow, chairman of the Earth Council Foundation, U.S., and board member of both the National Center for Geographic Information and Analysis, and the Institute for Global Environmental Strategies. He held various positions at the United Nations between 1971 and 1983, and has since served as senior advisor to Maurice Strong, secretary-general of the UN Conference on Environment and Development.
TU WEI-MING is director of the Harvard-Yenching Institute at Harvard University in Cambridge, Massachusetts. He is also a member of the Committee on the Study of Religion, chair of the Academia Sinica's advisory committee on the Institute of Chinese Literature and Philosophy, a fellow of the American Academy of Arts and Sciences, as well as a professor of Chinese history and philosophy.
JAMES J. WARD is director of international studies at Cedar Crest College in Allentown, Pennsylvania. He is also a professor of history and chair of the History and Political Science Department.
JANE TYLER WARD is associate dean of the faculty at Cedar Crest College in Allentown, Pennsylvania. She also supervises the English as a Second Language Program, and is an associate professor of psychology.
NEIL WATERS is a chair of the History Department and Kawashima Professor of Japanese Studies at Middlebury College in Middlebury, Vermont. He is also a member of the International Studies Steering Committee.
NEIL WEISSMAN is director of the Clarke Center for the Interdisciplinary Study of Contemporary Issues at Dickinson College in Carlisle, Pennsylvania. He is the former director of international education at the college, as well as a professor of history.
MARGARET SKILES ZELLJADT is an associate professor of German at Smith College in Northampton, Massachusetts. She is also a former director of the Smith College Junior Year in Hamburg, former associate dean for international study and a member of the Faculty Committee on Study Abroad.

ISBN 0-275-96045-5

90000>

9 780275 960452

HARDCOVER BAR CODE